Welcome to

There are some moments in history that steal news headlines and are remembered through the ages. But what about the forgotten intrigues and everyday oddities that have shaped our world? Transcending time periods and time zones, the Book of Weird History collates the strangest facts, stories and creations of all time. Tour memorable societies and meet eccentric characters, learning how their lives and lifestyles impacted the world as we know it. Fun and accessible, it will capture the imagination and give you a history lesson you won't forget.

All About History Book of

WEIRD HISTORY

Imagine Publishing Ltd
Richmond House
33 Richmond Hill
Bournemouth
Dorset BH2 6EZ
☎ +44 (0) 1202 586200
Website: www.imagine-publishing.co.uk
Twitter: @Books_Imagine
Facebook: www.facebook.com/ImagineBookazines

Publishing Director
Aaron Asadi

Head of Design
Ross Andrews

Editor in Chief
Jon White

Production Editor
Fiona Hudson

Senior Art Editor
Greg Whitaker

Assistant Designer
Sophie Ward

Photographer
James Sheppard

Printed by
William Gibbons, 26 Planetary Road, Willenhall, West Midlands, WV13 3XT

Distributed in the UK, Eire & the Rest of the World by
Marketforce, 5 Churchill Place, Canary Wharf, London, E14 5HU
Tel 0203 787 9060 www.marketforce.co.uk

Distributed in Australia by
Gordon & Gotch Australia Pty Ltd, 26 Rodborough Road, Frenchs Forest, NSW, 2086 Australia
Tel +61 2 9972 8800 www.gordongotch.com.au

IMAGINE
PUBLISHING

CONTENTS

17

23

16

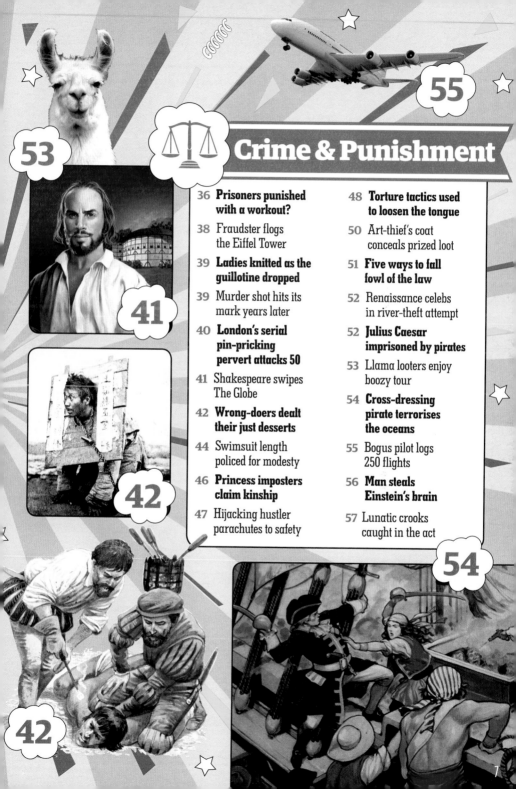

Crime & Punishment

55

53

41

42

54

42

7

86

62

73

Inventions & Discoveries

80

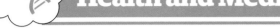

Health and Medicines

95

99

124

114

Sports, Art & Entertainment

118

LIFE & DEATH

14

15

17

23

12

16

AFTERLIFE ASSURED BY GRIM DEATH RITUAL

Eternal life wasn't just about preserving the spirit. The deceased's body also had to preserved, as the Ancient Egyptians believed the soul (*ba*) and life force (*ka*) had to return to it regularly to survive. To prevent the body from decaying, it underwent a lengthy and gruesome mummification process. Developed and refined over millennia, it allowed Ancient Egypt to produce some of the best-preserved mummies in the world, and we can now gaze upon the faces of men, women and children almost exactly as they were more than 2,000 years ago.

1. Purify the body
Before the embalming process can begin, the body is washed in water from the Nile and palm wine.

2. Remove the internal organs
A small incision is made in the left side of the body and the liver, lungs, intestines and stomach are removed. They are then washed and packed in natron before being placed in canopic jars. The heart is left in the body as it is believed to be the centre of intelligence, and will be needed in the afterlife.

5. Stuff the body
Once again, it is washed in water from the Nile and covered with oils to help the skin stay elastic. The natron is scooped out and the body is then stuffed with sawdust and linen to make it look lifelike.

3. Discard the brain
A rod is inserted through the nostril into the skull and used to break apart the brain so that it can drain out of the nose. The liquid is then thrown away as it is not thought to be useful.

4. Leave to dry
The body is stuffed and covered with natron, a type of salt, which will absorb any moisture. It is then left for 40 days to dry out.

The most complicated mummification process was developed in about 1550 BCE, and is considered the best method of preservation. During this method, the internal organs were removed, the flesh dehydrated, and the body wrapped in linen strips. This was an expensive process that took about 70 days to complete, so only the very rich could afford it. Working class people were treated with an alternative method of preservation that involved liquidising the internal organs with cedar tree oil, draining them out through the rectum and then placing the body in a salty substance called natron to dehydrate it.

Embalmers were skilled artisans who had a deep knowledge of anatomy and a steady hand. They were also often priests, as performing religious rites over the deceased was an equally important part of the embalming process. The most experienced priest carried out the major parts of mummification, like the wrapping of the body. He wore a jackal mask as he did so, symbolising the presence of Anubis, god of embalming and the afterlife.

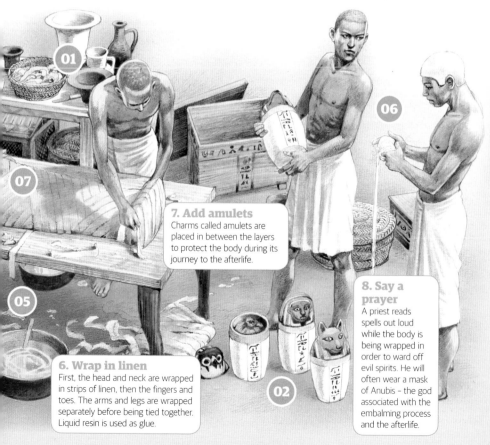

7. Add amulets
Charms called amulets are placed in between the layers to protect the body during its journey to the afterlife.

8. Say a prayer
A priest reads spells out loud while the body is being wrapped in order to ward off evil spirits. He will often wear a mask of Anubis – the god associated with the embalming process and the afterlife.

6. Wrap in linen
First, the head and neck are wrapped in strips of linen, then the fingers and toes. The arms and legs are wrapped separately before being tied together. Liquid resin is used as glue.

LOVE DUEL CONDUCTED VIA HOT AIR BALLOONS

■ A "very novel species of duel" - one of the most bizarre ever - took place in **19th-century Paris.** Monsieur de Grandpre and Monsieur de Pique, allegedly caught up in a love triangle, decided to duel in hot air balloons to show society that they were of a higher class. On 3 May 1808, each entered his hot air balloon with a primitive shotgun and a copilot to take the helm. De Pique fired first, but failed to hit his mark. De Grandpre was more accurate and his opponent's balloon deflated immediately, sending both passengers to their deaths.

WARTIME WEAPON DRIVES VICTIMS ITCHING MAD

The Norwegian resistance fighter responsible for the attack on brothel-goers

■ A powerful, nonlethal tool of war, itching powder would leave the opposition scratching like crazy. Archived instructions suggest: "The greatest effect is produced by applying the powder to the inside of the underclothing." Worse still, one case in 1944 saw itching powder used in contraceptives in military brothels, leading victims to believe they had fallen prey to a particularly nasty sexually transmitted disease. Either way, the results were pretty embarrassing!

Itching powder also had a more sinister side. Reports suggest an itching powder developed by scientists early in the war was incredibly strong and had the potential to make victims blind if it got into their eyes.

© Thinkstock

RAMESSES THE GREAT FATHERED 140

A pharaoh is expected to provide suitable heirs to the throne, and Ramesses the Great of Ancient Egypt approached this royal task with particular gusto. During the first ten years of his father Seti I's reign, a teenage Ramesses sired ten sons and at least as many daughters. Over the course of his long lifetime, Ramesses had six to eight principal wives, dozens of lesser wives and an untold number of concubines. He is believed to have fathered around 80 sons and 60 daughters - an impressive and somewhat excessive number, even by pharaoh standards.

Ramesses had good reason for spreading his seed. Although he was born into a common family, Ramesses was intent on reinstating a pure dynastic bloodline. He gave his male heirs high-ranking administrative posts and trained his first 12 sons as successors, but Ramesses outlived every one of them. The thirteenth son, Merenptah, assumed the throne around 1214 BCE but the Ramessid Dynasty withered away in only 150 years.

GENGHIS KHAN HAS 16 MILLION RELATIVES

■ **Claiming descent (often erroneously) from famous or powerful people has been a popular exercise throughout history.** But modern developments in DNA testing have revealed a vast number of people may in fact be directly related to Mongolian warrior king Genghis Khan. A 2003 study revealed that close to eight per cent of men living in the former Mongol Empire carry identical Y-chromosomes. That eight per cent is 0.5 per cent of the male worldwide population, which translates to a staggering 16 million descendants alive today. This lineage has been traced back to around 1,000 years ago, and the very special set of circumstances required for such a vast spread of DNA point to one man - a certain Genghis Khan. His empire spanned from Asia to the Caspian Sea and was characterised by widespread brutality and rape. The number of offspring his own sons boasted was staggering, with his eldest alone having a reported 40 sons and numerous daughters. Although this theory is impossible to ascertain without a sample of Khan's own DNA, it does seem likely that these identical chromosomes are linked in some way to Khan.

Great Khan's descendants include...

8% OF MEN LIVING IN THE FORMER MONGOL EMPIRE

16 MILLION WORLDWIDE (ALMOST DOUBLE THE POPULATION OF LONDON)

0.5% OF WORLDWIDE POPULATION

HUMBLE SAILOR SAVES ADMIRAL NELSON'S BACON

■ **At the Battle of Trafalgar in 1805, Admiral Lord Nelson's fleet defeated the French and Spanish navy.** It was a stunning victory in which the British didn't lose a single ship. Although Nelson himself was killed during the action, the battle cemented his legend.

Yet Nelson wouldn't have been there but for the bravery of a humble sailor several years earlier. By 1797, Nelson was a battle-hardened officer who had lost the sight in his right eye. Britain had been at war with France since 1793 and Rear Admiral Nelson was tasked with blockading the Spanish fleet at Cadiz. On 3 July 1797, he led a group of British boats in a night raid. Nelson's barge was involved in hand-to-hand combat with the crew of a Spanish boat and Nelson led from the front.

Seeing his superior in danger, Nelson's coxswain, John Sykes, put himself in the way of potentially fatal blows. Nelson later recalled the event: "This was a service hand-to-hand with swords, in which my coxswain John Sykes twice saved my life."

Sykes' heroics did not go unnoticed, with Nelson touting him for promotion, but he was killed in action a year later. Nelson made his mark on history but Britain came perilously close to their hero not even being there.

17

DEATH DEALT BY EXPLODING RODENTS

The exploding rat was one of the most ingenious inventions devised during World War II. The idea was that the rats would be skinned, filled with plastic explosives and sewn back up again. Still resembling rodents, albeit dead ones, the intention was to place them close to German boilers, such as those used on trains or on military bases. Left among the coal, unsuspecting Nazi soldiers would, it was expected, chuck them on to the fire, causing them to blow up.

The small amount of explosive would be amplified by the high pressure within the boiler and could cause a serious explosion. Not only would this prove to be shocking

and life-threatening for the opposition, the plan was that it would also destroy key infrastructure and inject panic among the German hierarchy and population. It was also assumed that it would take a while for the Germans to identify the culprit.

In the end, however, the exploding rodents were never used. A container full of dead rats was intercepted by the Germans, which alerted them to the wheeze. They subsequently spent many man-hours looking for more evidence of their use. "The trouble caused to them was a much greater success to us than if the rats had actually been used," the organisation that developed them concluded.

Exploding rats explained

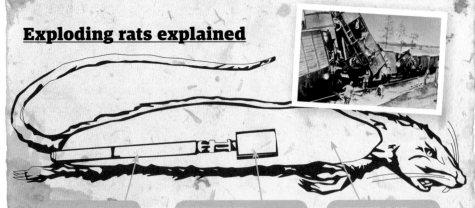

SAFETY FUSE
Leading out from the primer was a short length of safety fuse with a detonator on one end and a copper tube igniter on the other.

THE PRIMER
A standard No 6 primer was set within the plastic explosive. A primer is a small primary explosive device used to detonate a larger, less sensitive secondary explosive.

SKINNED RAT
Space needed to be created inside the rat in order to be filled with plastic explosive, so scientists skinned them and sewed them back up.

© Alamy; Thinkstock

DIAMOND RULER'S ESTATE ATTRACTS 470 CLAIMS

■ **The Nizam, or ruler, of Hyderabad – a princely state in India – Mir Osman Ali Khan became wealthy from mining diamonds in the late-19th century.** An eccentric man, he splashed his cash on a £50 million ($82.9 million) diamond the size of an ostrich egg, which he used as a paperweight, a 1.6-kilometre (one-mile)-long wardrobe full of silks and fine muslins, and filled an underground vault with broken trucks and lorries filled with gold coins and precious gems. But the Nizam's biggest vice was undoubtedly the opposite sex. He had a reported 86 mistresses and at least 100 illegitimate sons. Upon his death 470 of his descendants fought over £30 million ($49 million) left in a London bank account.

© Alamy

JAPANESE MAN SURVIVES DUAL ATOMIC BLASTS

■ **On 6 August 1945 a nuclear device exploded above the Japanese city of Hiroshima, killing approximately 130,000 people.** Among the survivors was Tsutomu Yamaguchi, who was in the city on business. He was three kilometres (1.8 miles) from the centre of the blast. Tsutomu suffered serious burns to his left side, damaged eardrums, and was temporarily blinded. He rested that night in an air-raid shelter but felt well enough to travel home the next day... to Nagasaki. Tsutomu was back to work on 9 August 1945 when a nuclear bomb was dropped on Nagasaki. An estimated 50,000 people died in that attack. Miraculously, Tsutomu Yamaguchi once again escaped death. The only person to have survived two nuclear attacks, he lived until 2010, aged 93.

JESUS' BIRTH DATE DECIDED BY CHURCH HEADS

Any study of the life of Jesus is bound to be contentious, raising a multitude of questions before any progress has been made. There is evidence to suggest that he did once live and that he was crucified by the Roman prefect of Judaea, Pontius Pilate. Things become more clouded, however, when we attempt to pin down the precise dates of his life. Although we can be fairly confident in saying he lived and died, there is absolutely no evidence to suggest that 25 December is anything more than just another day in the calendar.

Even the recently retired Pope Benedict XVI has disputed the exact birth date of Christ, suggesting that the sixth-century monk Dionysius Exiguus may have made an error in his calculations. The Pope agreed with the popular belief that Jesus was, in fact, born between six and four BCE. While we can make an approximation of the year of Jesus' birth, pinning down the day proves somewhat more difficult. This is because the Bible does not provide any dates for this event - or even a season. The closest thing to a clue we get is the shepherds tending their flocks by night, suggesting the weather was cold.

The decision to anoint 25 December as Christ's birthday stems from around 300 CE, when Christianity was still trying to establish itself as the dominant religion in the Roman Empire. Christian leaders observed the popularity of pagan rituals and realised they needed to create their own annual celebration. The appointed date of Christmas is extremely close to the pagan celebration of Yule, which occurs on 21 December, and directly overlaps with the Roman festival of Saturnalia and the Iranian celebration of the birth of Mithras, the Sun of Righteousness.

After some debate about whether the day should be glorified at all, the first celebration of Christ's birth took place in Rome in 336 CE.

SAFETY COFFINS GUARDED VICTORIAN UNDEAD

▨ **Very much a historical oddity, the life-preserving coffin was a special burial casket that would allow those mistakenly buried alive to safely get out.**

Designed by Christian Henry Eisenbrandt in 1843, the system worked by fitting the typical hinged lid with a series of levers and springs, which activated via motion-detecting devices in the coffin, ultimately releasing the latch.

Any motion was detected through two mechanisms: a ring slipped around the occupant's finger and a metal head plate. Both were connected by wires to the coffin's opening mechanism, and the slightest movement would trigger the lid catch.

In addition to the opening mechanism, the life-preserving coffin also featured a mesh in its lid which would supposedly provide a limited supply of air post-burial.

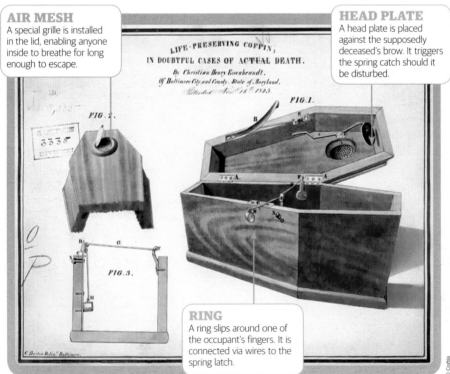

AIR MESH
A special grille is installed in the lid, enabling anyone inside to breathe for long enough to escape.

HEAD PLATE
A head plate is placed against the supposedly deceased's brow. It triggers the spring catch should it be disturbed.

LIFE-PRESERVING COFFIN, IN DOUBTFUL CASES OF ACTUAL DEATH.
By Christian Henry Eisenbrandt.
Of Baltimore City and County, State of Maryland.
Patented Nov. 15th 1843.

FIG.1.

FIG.2.

FIG.3.

RING
A ring slips around one of the occupant's fingers. It is connected via wires to the spring latch.

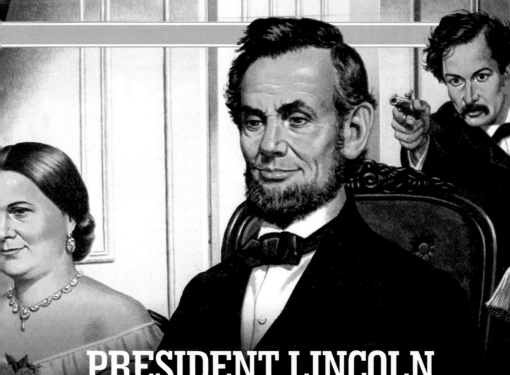

PRESIDENT LINCOLN PREDICTED HIS OWN DEATH

■ **According to Lincoln's friend Ward Hill Lamon, three days prior to his assassination on 14 April 1865 the president recounted a strange dream he had had the previous week.** Lamon retold the tale in his biography of Lincoln entitled *Recollections of Abraham Lincoln 1847-1865*, in which he described how Lincoln stated that in his dream he woke in the White House to the sound of weeping.

After progressing from room to room and finding 'no living person in sight', Lincoln entered the East Room and discovered a large catafalque with a corpse laid upon it, shrouded in funeral vestments. Surrounding the scene were a selection of soldiers and large group of mourners, who were the source of the sobbing. Lincoln continued to reveal that he approached the

corpse and asked one of the soldiers "Who is dead in the White House?" After a pause the soldier replied, "The President, he was killed by an assassin."

Many commentators in the past have added prophetic qualities to this event, however perhaps it merely reveals the great and very real strain the president was under during that time. Numerous real-life death threats had been received by the president and, with the tumultuous state of America following the bloody and destructive civil war, an attempt on his life had been a very real possibility that may have occupied his mind.

Lincoln would never know the timeliness of his dream; within three days of recounting it to Lamon he was indeed assassinated by John Wilkes Booth.

HEADLESS CHICKEN DEFIES DEATH

■ **The survival of Mike the Chicken after having his head wiped clean off his body still continues to amaze.** Farmer Lloyd Olsen had already swung his axe to kill 40 chickens that day in 1945, but Mike was like none of the others. Somehow the blade did not completely sever the jugular vein, and after the blow was landed, Mike simply stood back up and got on like nothing had happened. A few days later it became clear that the chicken wasn't giving up the ghost just yet, so Olsen and his wife continued to feed and water him using a pipette.

To find out why Mike survived, he was taken to the University of Utah. It turned out that the brain stem had remained in tact, meaning that Mike was acting in the same way as a brain-dead human – hence why he was still able to carry out the most basic functions. Back on the farm, local residents got wind of the amazing animal and the Olsens began charging spectators a quarter to see him. Mike the Chicken lived on for another 18 months, and became a minor celebrity in the process.

FRANZ FERDINAND KILLED 300,000 ANIMALS

■ **Being a crown prince of Bohemia gave Franz almost exclusive access to vast hunting grounds – and he was a zealous hunter.** Franz's diaries make note of around 300,000 kills of various game species, including 5,000 deer. Around 100,000 of these were stuffed and put on display in his Czech castle. He would request a hunting trip on every official excursion and would often challenge sharpshooters to shooting contests. Not surprisingly, he frequently won.

© Corbis/Getty Images

DAILY HUMAN SACRIFICES OFFERED TO AZTEC GODS

How many?
The Aztec civilisation had around 10 million subjects. Constant human sacrifices meant the number of victims was huge – probably the greatest number in human history.

Who?
One male and one female priest would officiate. They would develop good anatomical skills in the process of removing skin and organs.

Why?
Human sacrifice was conducted to please the Aztec gods, not out of bloodlust but for continued prosperity. Sacrificial victims frequently went to their deaths willingly, having been promised great riches in the next life.

How?
Aztec warriors attempted to capture their enemies alive. A number of horrific methods were documented: hearts removed and shown to the Sun; flayed alive and skin worn by priests; or even boiled in huge vats. It was believed to be important to ingest the essence of fallen enemies.

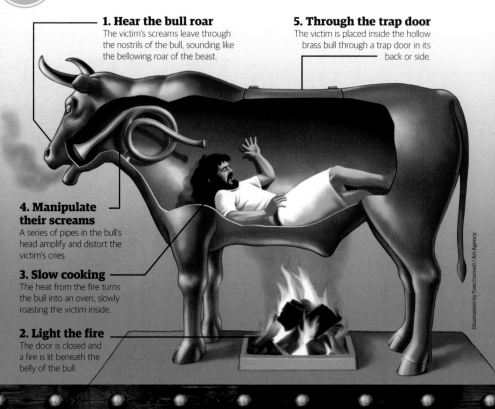

1. Hear the bull roar
The victim's screams leave through the nostrils of the bull, sounding like the bellowing roar of the beast.

5. Through the trap door
The victim is placed inside the hollow brass bull through a trap door in its back or side.

4. Manipulate their screams
A series of pipes in the bull's head amplify and distort the victim's cries.

3. Slow cooking
The heat from the fire turns the bull into an oven, slowly roasting the victim inside.

2. Light the fire
The door is closed and a fire is lit beneath the belly of the bull.

Illustration by Tom Connell / Art Agency

AUDIENCES DELIGHT AT DEATH HOWLS

■ **One of the most brutal methods of execution ever created took the form of the Brazen Bull.** Invented in ancient Greece by Perillus, a bronze worker in Athens, it was given as a gift to a cruel tyrant named Phalaris of Agrigentum. As well as roasting criminals alive, the device also doubled as a musical instrument, converting the victim's desperate cries into what Perillus described as "the tenderest, most pathetic, most melodious of bellowings". Distrustful of the inventor's claims, Phalaris ordered Perillus to climb inside and prove the device's musical capabilities himself.

As soon as Perillus was inside, Phalaris shut the door and lit a fire beneath, causing Perillus to scream for real. However, rather then letting him die at the hands of his own creation, Phalaris had the inventor removed and thrown off a cliff instead.

VLAD THE IMPALER WASHED HIS HANDS IN BLOOD

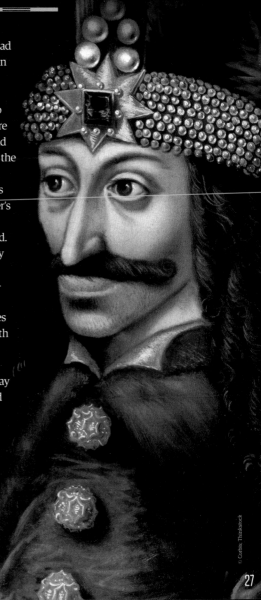

■ **There is no doubt that Bram Stoker's historical muse enjoyed spilling blood.** Vlad Dracul ruled Wallachia, one of the three main provinces of modern Romania, on three occasions between 1448 and 1476.

As ruler, his father had been inducted into the Order of the Dragon, created by the future Holy Roman Emperor Sigismund in 1408 and tasked with defending Christendom against the Ottoman Turks. In their youth, Vlad and his brother Radu had spent six years as hostages of the Turkish Murad II to ensure their father's loyalty. It is probable he witnessed brutal impalements by the Turks during this period.

Upon ascending the throne, Vlad routinely used impalement to punish aristocrats and peasants alike. Stories circulated in late-15th-century Europe of Vlad Dracul dipping his bread in the blood of his victims. Such stories would have strengthened his association with the vampire, a folkloric undead creature in the legends of Romania and the Balkans. A German poem from the time does not portray Vlad as a blood drinker, but claims he would wash his hands in his victims' blood before taking his dinner.

After being killed in a battle outside Bucharest on 26 December 1476, Vlad's severed head was presented to Sultan Mehmet II on a pole. It is possible this may have contributed to the legend that a vampire must have its head cut off to be fully vanquished.

ITALIAN KNIGHT BURSTS INTO FLAMES

■ **Death by spontaneous combustion is the stuff of nightmares, confined to horror stories of yore.** Yet it's a demise that one poor Italian knight succumbed to in the 1400s. After quaffing a few glasses of strong wine, Polonus Vorstius began to feel unwell, and proceeded to burp long flames of fire. Soon, the flames consumed his entire body. Nobody knows for certain what causes spontaneous human combustion, but it's a well-documented cause of death throughout history, with more than 200 cases recorded in the last 300 years alone.

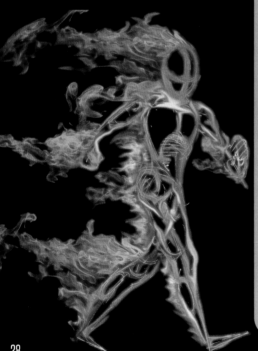

GHOSTBUSTER HOUDINI OUTS QUACKS

■ **Appalled to see the innovations he had used to entertain being twisted, Harry Houdini attended séances in disguise to debunk mediums.** Sometimes it was all too easy; when one claimed to have summoned the ghost of Abraham Lincoln, the well-read Houdini simply asked questions about the President's life that the fraud was unable to answer correctly.

Other mediums offered Houdini a greater test of his cunning and on one occasion he wore a tight bandage on his knee all day in order to make his skin extremely sensitive to the slightest movement. It was incredibly painful but when he attended the séance he was able to feel the medium fumbling around under the table for her props.

© Dreamstime

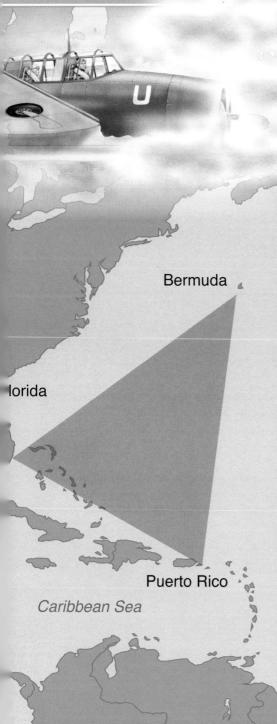

AIRCRAFT AWOL IN ATLANTIC DEADZONE

Bermuda

lorida

Puerto Rico

Caribbean Sea

■ **Between Florida, Puerto Rico and Bermuda rests a body of sea that's baffled scientists for centuries.** Encompassing approximately 710,000 kilometres of sea, this deceptively large patch of ocean, known as the Bermuda Triangle, is notorious for disappearances. On average, four planes and 20 boats go missing in the area every year, but the debris is never found.

The first report of strange goings on in the Bermuda Triangle comes from Christopher Columbus, who, on 8 October 1492, wrote in his diaries that his compasses stopped working in the area. He also wrote of seeing a fireball in the sky.

The most famous disappearance in the Bermuda Triangle happened in 1945. Five planes known as 'Flight 19' were lost over the area, as well as the search plane sent to rescue the original lost crew. In total, six planes and 27 men were lost.

It's only now that the enigma of the Bermuda Triangle seems to be cracking. Many have claimed alien and UFO involvement, though methane hydrates are currently the most likely explanation. Human error is another likely cause, as the Bermuda Triangle is one of only two places in the world where compasses point true north rather than magnetic north.

DOG DEATH BRIDGE CLAIMS 50 POOCHES

Bridges with bad reputations aren't something you stumble upon every day, but Overtoun Bridge in Scotland is one such structure. Infamous for its canine suicides, more than 50 dogs have leapt over the bridge's walls and plummeted to their deaths, and plenty others have risked their lives in a similar way.

The enduring mystery of Scotland's spooky suicide bridge continues, and neither scientists nor psychologists have been able to wrap their heads around what it is that drives dogs to take the leap. Some locals claim that it's the work of the 'White Lady of Overtoun', a ghostly figure from the nearby manor house. Others claim that it's simply curiosity that killed the dog.

One recent theory seems a likely explanation, and scientists have performed experiments to back up their idea. Minks that live in the undergrowth surrounding and underneath the bridge give off a smell that's utterly irresistible to dogs, so it is thought that they are simply following their noses to the source.

In any case, the tarnished reputation of the bridge has prompted local authorities to put up signs warning dog owners of the bridge's dangers. A sign reading "Dangerous bridge: Please keep your dog on a lead" now marks the spot of many dogs' last steps.

SURVIVOR REFUSES TO GO DOWN WITH THE SHIP(S)

When Violet Jessop was diagnosed with tuberculosis as a child, the doctors gave her months to live. Little did they know that not only would she survive this illness, she would also go on to survive three maritime disasters.

In 1910, Violet took a job as a stewardess on RMS Olympic. The following year, it collided with a warship, but all those on board lived to tell the tale.

In 1912, Violet set sail on RMS Titanic. When the ship hit an iceberg four days later, she was one of the lucky few that made it into a lifeboat.

Then in 1916, Violet survived yet another tragedy after an unexplained explosion sank the RMS Britannic. 'Miss Unsinkable' finally died in 1971, at the ripe old age of 83.

TAXI DUO IN KILLER CRASH DEJA VU

In 1975, 17-year-old Erskine Ebbin was killed while riding his moped on the island of Bermuda. Unbelievably, the taxi involved was same vehicle that had struck and killed his 17-year-old brother Neville the year before. According to reports, the accident involved the same driver carrying the same passenger, on the same intersection and both brothers rode the very same moped! Some even say the accidents occurred exactly one year apart.

Too strange to be true? Probably. But analysts have noted that as Bermuda is a small island with a small population, the likelihood of this weird coincidence occurring was slim but possible all the same.

© Thinkstock

31

LONG-LOST TWINS LEAD IDENTICAL LIVES

◼ **Identical twins sharing lives is nothing new, but how about a pair of identical twins brought up by different families?** In one case, the twin bond certainly prevailed. Twins Jim Springer and Jim Lewis were both named James by their adopted families, both had a childhood dog named 'Toy' and they were raised in the suburbs of Ohio within just 72 kilometres (45 miles) of one another.

But the similarities don't end there. As adults, both married twice (first to a woman called Linda, then to a Betty), had a first son named James Allen, drove Chevrolets and served as sheriffs for separate counties in their home state. They eventually found each other and discovered their strange sibling connection at the age of 39 - a huge turning point in both of their lives.

HENRY VIII: DEAD KING'S CORPSE EXPLODES

◼ **Did you know that Henry VIII's corpse became so bloated in the days following his death that it actually exploded?** The cause of such a fate - and his weight gain in his later years - began in a jousting accident in his youth, in which Henry struck his head and damaged his pituitary gland.

The king became so obese as a result that he could barely move. When he died in 1547, a lead-lined coffin capable of containing his extreme girth was built. Alas, the build up of gasses inside his body became too much, and it ruptured in transit.

It is said that before the mess could be cleaned up, many dogs made a dinner of the Henry's leaked insides!

© Thinkstock

HISTORY'S FREAKIEST FATALITIES

They say always wear clean underwear to avoid embarrassment in case you get hit by a bus. But for these unfortunate souls, the state of their underwear was the least of their worries. Perishing in unlikely circumstances, the final moments of these characters ensured they would never be forgotten.

Accidental suicide

19th-century lawyer Clement Vallandigham accidentally shot himself while trying to demonstrate how another man may have done the same. Although he died from his wounds, he had proved his point and the defendant was acquitted.

Death at the reins

In 1923, jockey Frank Hayes suffered a heart attack halfway through a race and died, but his body remained attached to the saddle. His horse finished first, making him the only jockey to have won a race after death.

The Great Molasses Flood

On 15 January 1919, at a distilling factory in Boston, a huge tank of molasses burst open, sending a wave of sweet, gloopy liquid rushing through the streets. 21 people were killed and 150 injured.

The peckish chemist

Swedish chemist Carl Wilhelm Scheele had a bad habit of sniffing and tasting every new substance he discovered. He died at the age of 43, and his premature demise was blamed on overexposure to mercury, arsenic and lead.

Bitten by death

When Viking warrior Sigurd Eysteinsson beheaded an enemy, he strapped the severed head to his horse. While riding, the teeth grazed against Sigurd's leg and the wound became infected, ultimately resulting in his death.

CRIME & PUNISHMENT

53

PRISONERS PUNISHED WITH A WORKOUT

■ **Many Victorian prisons were fitted with a treadmill, upon which prisoners would spend hours grinding flour in order to earn their keep.** In one gruelling eight-hour shift, prisoners would climb the equivalent of 2,200m (7,200ft). By the end of the 19th century, the task of grinding grain had been handed over to factories, but the prisons kept their treadmills and used them as a form of punishment.

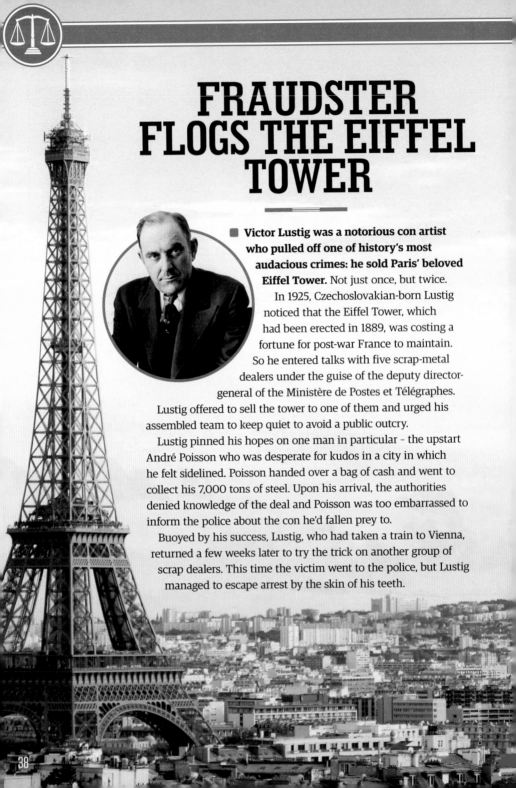

FRAUDSTER FLOGS THE EIFFEL TOWER

Victor Lustig was a notorious con artist who pulled off one of history's most audacious crimes: he sold Paris' beloved Eiffel Tower. Not just once, but twice.

In 1925, Czechoslovakian-born Lustig noticed that the Eiffel Tower, which had been erected in 1889, was costing a fortune for post-war France to maintain. So he entered talks with five scrap-metal dealers under the guise of the deputy director-general of the Ministère de Postes et Télégraphes. Lustig offered to sell the tower to one of them and urged his assembled team to keep quiet to avoid a public outcry.

Lustig pinned his hopes on one man in particular – the upstart André Poisson who was desperate for kudos in a city in which he felt sidelined. Poisson handed over a bag of cash and went to collect his 7,000 tons of steel. Upon his arrival, the authorities denied knowledge of the deal and Poisson was too embarrassed to inform the police about the con he'd fallen prey to.

Buoyed by his success, Lustig, who had taken a train to Vienna, returned a few weeks later to try the trick on another group of scrap dealers. This time the victim went to the police, but Lustig managed to escape arrest by the skin of his teeth.

LADIES KNITTED AS THE GUILLOTINE DROPPED

■ **In France, the word 'tricoteuse' can apply to any lady who likes to knit, but in the 18th century it conjured far more sinister images**. As the flames of the French Revolution were stoked, thousands of working-class women took to the streets to protest the high food prices and chronic shortages. At first they were praised by the government, but over the years their rowdy behaviour became an annoyance and they were banned from attending political assemblies. Instead, they made their presence known by quietly knitting beside the guillotine in the Place de la Revolution, watching as head after head rolled.

MURDER SHOT HITS ITS MARK YEARS LATER

■ **In 1893, Henry Ziegland's breakup went seriously awry.** After his ex committed suicide, her brother sought vengeance, gun in hand. Ziegland was not fatally wounded; the bullet skimmed past and became lodged in the tree behind him. As time passed, Ziegland became known as the luckiest man in the land, having escaped his would-be killer.

20 years passed and Ziegland's mind turned to the tree that took his bullet. He decided that it was time to get rid of it. The tree was thick, and Ziegland found that he couldn't saw through it on his own. Instead, he surrounded the tree with explosives and blew it up. Having been concealed for two decades, the bullet soared out of the tree. In an incredible twist of fate, the bullet destined for Ziegland 20 years earlier hit its intended mark, killing him instantly.

© Getty Images

LONDON'S SERIAL PIN-PRICKING PERVERT ATTACKS 50

■ **Between 1788 and 1790, London was terrorised by a serial stabber.** His weapon of choice? A pin. Attacking only women, more than 50 victims claimed to have been attacked by what the papers dubbed the 'London Monster'.

Over the course of two years, many women of high society reported being attacked by a man who had stabbed them in the bottom, though other, more brutal accounts claimed that ladies had been stabbed with a knife. After a few reports, a trend emerged; it became clear that the attacker had a 'type', choosing victims who were all renowned beauties.

Reported cases spiked, with some women claiming to have been victimised by the London Monster to boost their own appeal in society - some women even going so far as to fake injuries.

In 1790, an unemployed man called Rhynwick Williams was arrested for the crimes, although to this day many people question his involvement - or whether the London Monster was a case of hysteria or even a real person at all...

© Alamy

SHAKESPEARE SWIPES THE GLOBE

Before the Globe, London's most celebrated theatre was situated on the north side of the River Thames in Shoreditch. Aptly named 'The Theatre', it was built by James Burbage and for decades had been home to many acting troupes including the Lord Chamberlain's Men, of which Shakespeare was a part.

The land was leased from a Mr Allen, but in 1597 he refused to renew the contract. After months of disagreements, Burbage's sons decided to take matters into their own hands. In the dead of night, the two men, along with a carpenter and a dozen actors, "armed with unlawful and offensive weapons, as namely swords, daggers, bills, axes and such like", crept onto the site and dismantled the theatre. Shakespeare was one of them.

As the Burbages couldn't afford to lease a new plot on their own, they offered five members of the company the chance to become part-owners of a new theatre. With their investments, they leased some land on the south bank of the river and ferried the salvaged timber to Southwark. The materials were used to build another, and in 1599 the Globe Theatre opened its doors to the public.

WRONG-DOERS DEALT THEIR JUST DESSERTS

■ **Authorities have tried many tactics over the centuries to punish the misdeeds of society's naughtiest inhabitants.** But when the prisons are full to bursting and there are dastardly deeds that still to be punished, police forces resorted to some very odd techniques. Ingenious, inhumane and often odd solutions were used to forge a safer society. Pain, humiliation and rehabilitation: all of the above have been used to dish out a lesson guaranteed not to be forgotten.

Drunkard's cloak
16th century

The drunkard's cloak was a beer barrel with a hole for the offender's head and two smaller holes in the sides for the arms. Once suitably attired, the miscreant was paraded through the town. Not surprisingly, this was a punishment for those convicted of drunkenness, something Puritans were keen to address during the Commonwealth. Newcastle must have had a particular problem, as the drunkard's cloak was often linked to that area – some sources describe it as the 'Newcastle cloak'.

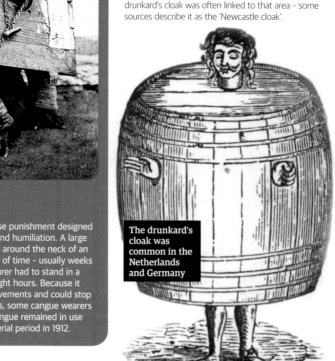

The drunkard's cloak was common in the Netherlands and Germany

Cangue
2nd century BCE

The cangue was a Chinese punishment designed to inflict both hardship and humiliation. A large wooden board was fixed around the neck of an offender for a set period of time – usually weeks or months – and the wearer had to stand in a public place during daylight hours. Because it restricted a person's movements and could stop them feeding themselves, some cangue wearers starved to death. The cangue remained in use until the end of the imperial period in 1912.

Ducking stool
1597

The ducking stool was a chair fastened to a long beam on the edge of a pond or river. An offender would be strapped in and dropped into the water. It was a variation on the earlier cucking stool, which was mainly used as a method of humiliation. It was usually reserved for women, often those convicted of scolding their husbands. The last recorded British ducking took place in 1809.

Ducking stools were also used in Medieval times to try to identify witches

Branding iron
1st century BCE

Brand marks have been used as a punishment for centuries. This method combines the pain of physical punishment with the permanent public humiliation of being identified as a criminal. Thieves and runaway slaves were marked by the Romans, and English Medieval courts used a number of different marks: V for vagrants, S for runaway slaves, B for blasphemers and F for affray (fraymakers). Branding was outlawed in Britain in 1829 and has mostly died out across the world.

© Thinkstock

43

SWIMSUIT LENGTH POLICED FOR MODESTY

■ **A police officer measures the length of the female bathing fashion in Atlantic City, New Jersey.** Swimwear had once covered the whole female figure, but by the time of this photograph in 1921, attitudes had begun to change. Swimsuits were now armless one-piece garments, and this new maillot style was a far cry from the long bathing dresses of the 19th century.

PRINCESS IMPOSTERS CLAIM KINSHIP

■ **So what became of Princess Anastasia?** Famously the youngest daughter of Russian Tsar Nicholas II, Anastasia's fate became enshrined in myth after the brutal execution of her entire family by the Bolshevik secret police in 1918. Her body was found to be missing from the burial site of her parents and three sisters, prompting rumours of her escape. Several women subsequently came forward to claim their royal kinship. The discovery of her remains in 2007 would prove all of them frauds.

Nadezhda Vasilyeva

Vasilyeva appeared in Siberia in 1920 while travelling to China and was arrested by the authorities. She sent letters to the British King George V pleading for his help. In 1971, she died in an insane asylum in the city of Kazan. The head of the hospital claimed that "except for her claim that she was Anastasia, she was completely sane."

Eugenia Smith

Though not as famous as Anderson, Smith wrote *Autobiography Of HIH Anastasia Nicholaevna Of Russia* in 1963. In the book Smith recounts in great detail what life was like in the Russian Imperial family up until their execution. She eventually distanced herself from the claim and is said to have refused a DNA test shortly before her death in 1997.

Anna Anderson

During the 1920s, Anna (a Pole called Franziska Schanzkowska) appeared in Germany claiming to be Anastasia. Her lack of Russian and rebuttals by Romanov relatives undermined her case but she received support from Rasputin's daughter. The most famous of the imposters, her story inspired a 1956 film starring Ingrid Bergman.

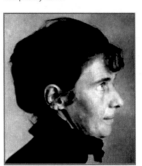

HIJACKING HUSTLER PARACHUTES TO SAFETY

■ **The true identity of 'DB Cooper' – the man who exited his own holdup via parachute – continues to baffle.** On Thanksgiving Eve in 1971, a man who identified himself as 'Dan Cooper' boarded Flight 305 to Seattle on a one-way ticket. The unassuming man in the black suit ordered bourbon, lit a cigarette and passed a note to a flight attendant. It read: "I have a bomb in my briefcase. I will use it if necessary. I want you to sit next to me. You are being hijacked."

His demands? Cooper declared he wanted $200,000 (equivalent to £680,000/$1,160,000 today), four parachutes and a fuel truck waiting for the plane's arrival. The flight attendant relayed his orders to ground control and the aeroplane circled over Washington for two hours while the president of Northwest Orient worked with local authorities to meet Cooper's demands.

With everything in place, the plane touched down on an isolated part of McChord Air Force Base. The money and parachutes were exchanged for the hostages, then the refuelled plane took to the skies once again. Cooper directed the pilots to cruise toward Mexico City at the slowest air speed possible without stalling. At around 8pm Cooper opened the craft's staircase and leapt from the plane, parachuting to freedom. He and the money are never seen again.

TORTURE TACTICS USED TO LOOSEN THE TONGUE

■ **Humanity's penchant for cruelty is captured perfectly in its tools of torture.** These horrific devices were used to break mind and body in pursuit of information or a confession. But torture was often ineffective; desperate for relief, victims would often say whatever they thought would make the pain stop.

Iron maiden
1793

The iron maiden was a torture device in which a victim was encased within a spiked coffin. Historians today believe that despite the device being often associated with the Middle Ages, it was in fact a later creation, with no record of it found earlier than the late-18th century. Regardless of its origin, the iron maiden was a fearsome tool, capable of wounding or killing with ease. Today, many historians believe the device was used more as a mental torture tool, with victims threatened with its use rather than actually encased within it.

Waterboarding
2002

While waterboarding has been in use for centuries, its most modern incarnation was introduced by the USA following the 11 September attacks in 2001. The method involves pouring water into the nose and mouth of a victim who is forced to lie on their back on an inclined platform. This simulates the feeling of drowning and can cause brain damage through oxygen deprivation. This practice was not considered torture according to the US Department of Justice, and it permitted the Central Intelligence Agency (CIA) to use the technique against any suspected terrorist.

Bamboo torture 1941

One of the East's most ingenious and horrific torture techniques, bamboo torture entailed tying a victim up with ropes above a patch of bamboo – often on a wooden frame – before leaving them to be impaled by the plant's sharp and incredibly fast-growing shoots. The shoots would first puncture the victim's skin and then penetrate further, horrifically skewering them and making them bleed to death. This torture technique was reportedly used by Japanese soldiers during WWII, but records show the technique was also utilised in China and Malaysia prior to that date.

Thumbscrew 1250

Also known as 'the pillywinks', this was a simple vice-like device that allowed a victim's thumbs to be slowly crushed or dislocated. The instrument worked by trapping the victim's thumbs beneath a metal bar, which was then slowly squeezed down by a butterfly clamp. Despite being invented in Medieval Europe, the thumbscrew remained such a popular torture implement that it was still being used by the 19th century. Records indicated it was often used to punish slaves for relatively minor indiscretions.

Twisting the thumbscrew left victims writhing in pain

Crucifixion 600 BCE

Despite being made famous as a capital punishment, notably in the crucifixion of Jesus, the practice of crucifixion is one of the earliest recorded forms of torture. Developed by the ancient Persians, Seleucids and Carthaginians in the 6th century BCE, crucifixion involved whipping a victim, often forcing them to drag a large wooden crossbeam to the place of their punishment, then binding or nailing them to it. The the beam was then hoisted up a vertical shaft to a height of three metres (ten feet). This would levy intense and prolonged pain on the crucified, which would lead to death by exhaustion or heart failure.

© Alamy, Thinkstock

Heretic's fork 1478

An early example of sleep-deprivation torture, the heretic's fork forced its victim to remain conscious at all times. The heretic's fork was a double-ended, two-pronged metal fork that would be strapped around the victim's neck, with one fork placed on the throat and the other fork placed on the breastbone. The victim was then hung from the ceiling, preventing them from lying down. As such, the victim was forced to remain conscious, and as soon as their head dropped from fatigue they would impale themselves. This torture tool was a favourite of the Spanish Inquisition.

ART-THIEF'S COAT CONCEALS PRIZED LOOT

■ **The art world's biggest heist earned its perpetrator, Stéphane Breitwieser, a cool $1.4 billion.** Self-proclaimed art connoisseur Breitwieser's career as an art thief began in Germany in 1995 and ended in 2001, during which time he 'collected' 239 works of art from 172 museums across Europe. His method was cunning, yet simple. An accomplice - his girlfriend - would distract security guards while Breitwieser would simply lift the artwork off the walls and stash them under his coat. Breitwieser's crime spree only came to an end in 2001, when he was caught stealing a bugle from the Richard Wagner Museum in Switzerland.

Breitwieser was only sentenced to three years in prison, serving just two. Justifying the short sentence, authorities noted that the robbery wasn't motivated by profit; Breitwieser simply wanted to keep the art for himself. After leaving prison, he gained fame with his 2006 autobiography, *Confessions d'un Voleur d'Art* (Confessions Of An Art Thief).

Breitwieser's mother destroyed the masterpieces to protect her son

© Alamy, Thinkstock

FIVE WAYS TO FALL FOWL OF THE LAW

■ **As times change, so too do the laws.** Today we may find it reasonable to deem certain offences 'criminal' that were once practised freely and sanctioned by authorities. So too can we look back in time and laugh at nonsensical laws that were once strictly enforced for the good of society. Some such laws have somehow survived. You won't believe the rules that are in place in the modern world...

Avoid death

It is illegal to die in the Houses of Parliament in Britain. Anyone who dies here is entitled to a state funeral, so the law was put in place to prevent it from ever happening.

No gum-dealers

After authorities became infuriated with the improper disposal of gum, Singapore passed a law in 2004 prohibiting the sale of chewing gum, though it's still legal to chew it.

Don't wear trousers

In place since the 1800s and yet to be repealed, a French law states that it is illegal for women to wear trousers. Fortunately two amendments made in the late-19th century mean there are exceptions to the rule – but only while riding or cycling!

Leave your armour at home

Thanks to a law passed during the reign of Edward II in England, it is illegal for anyone to enter the Houses of Parliament in a full suit of armour. In fact, it's worded so that kevlar vests and guns are forbidden too.

Don't knock on doors

Preventing nuisance behaviour, an 1839 Metropolitan Police Act forbids children from knocking on doors without any cause (aka 'cherry knocking'). The act also forbids anyone from flying kites, beating doormats and blowing horns.

RENAISSANCE CELEBS IN RIVER-THEFT ATTEMPT

■ **How does anyone steal a river?** Answer: you don't. The dynamic duo of Leonardo da Vinci and Niccolo Machiavelli walked away with nothing but red cheeks and a pile of dirt after their audacious attempt to steal the River Arno flopped. While in the employ of the nefarious Cesare Borgia, Machiavelli convinced da Vinci to aid him in Cesare's plan to divert the river away from the city of Pisa, Florence's closest military rival. Success would have meant Florence would have been bolstered by incoming sea trade. Despite da Vinci's brilliant plan to reroute the river with dams and artificial inlets, the operation proved too costly and da Vinci tasted failure. You've got to admire their guts, though.

JULIUS CAESAR IMPRISONED BY PIRATES

■ **When Rome's most powerful dictator was captured by Cilician pirates in the Aegean sea, he proved that he was a force to be reckoned with.** Upon demanding a ransom of 20 silver talents, Caesar laughed in their faces and suggested they asked for 50 instead. Confused, the pirates agreed, and Caesar sent his men to fetch the ransom. Now alone with some of the most feared men in the empire, rather than cowering he took to treating them as his subordinates. He joined them in their games and exercises, and silenced them when he wanted to take a nap. When his men returned with the silver over a month later and set him free, Caesar immediately ordered for all of the pirates to be crucified.

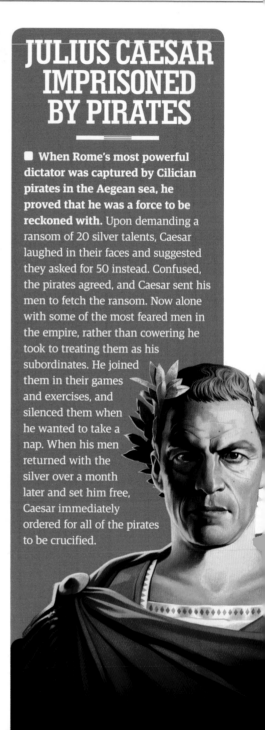

In 2013, one lucky llama experienced a guided tour of the French city of Bordeaux before being returned home by authorities.

Five teenagers on a night out initially planned to borrow a zebra from a nearby circus, but admitted that while the zebra was too stubborn to join them, the llama - named Serge - seemed more than happy to go along for the ride.

The group of men, who had left a nightclub close to the circus, took Serge around the city, even on a tram ride. It was only when the tram driver called the police that the men left Serge tied to a lamp post - but not before taking a few pictures with their four-legged friend.

Serge was returned to the circus safe and sound, but the circus responded by upping security around the animal enclosures.

The five men were later arrested, but a petition was launched, calling for the group of men not to face any criminal charges.

LLAMA LOOTERS ENJOY BOOZY TOUR

© Thinkstock

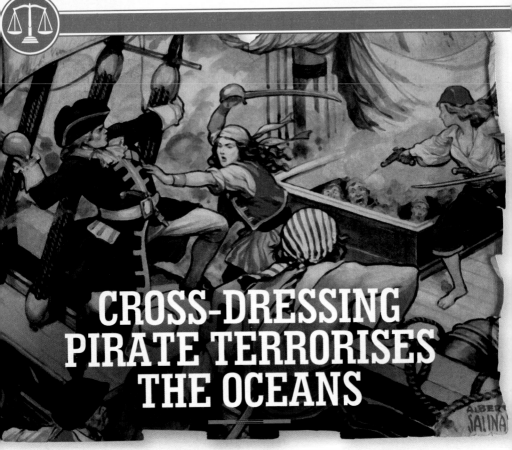

CROSS-DRESSING PIRATE TERRORISES THE OCEANS

■ **Female buccaneers were far from unheard of during the golden age of piracy.** But that didn't stop Mary Read from dressing as a man for most of her ocean-going career. In fact, she was raised as a boy by her widowed mother in order that they could continue living on an allowance intended for her dead older brother. Read took his place in disguise, and even her grandmother was none the wiser to the ruse throughout Read's teenage years.

Continuing to hide her gender, Read joined the British military and gained a reputation as a ferocious fighter during the War of Spanish Succession. She did eventually marry and settle down, running an inn with her husband in the Netherlands for a time. But when he died she donned her old attire and resumed her military career. That was until a ship she was aboard was taken by pirates en route to the West Indies. Read joined them immediately.

Hooking up with 'Calico' Jack Rackham in 1720, she formed a close friendship with Jack's partner Anne Bonny - the only other woman known to have been convicted of piracy during its heyday. They were involved in the plunder of several vessels before Rackham and his crew were captured and taken to Jamaica for trial and execution.

Read and Bonny had actually put up a vicious fight, berating their male colleagues for not doing likewise, but they were outmatched. Read, having escaped the noose by pleading pregnancy, eventually died in prison of a fever.

BOGUS PILOT LOGS 250 FLIGHTS

■ **Frank Abagnale is one of the world's most respected authorities on forgery and embezzlement, but in his youth, he was one of America's most wanted fraudsters.** At the age of 15, Abagnale's own father became his first victim after the lad used his credit card to exchange car parts for cash. Over the next few years, Abagnale opened several accounts with different banks and wrote out cheques to himself, encouraging them to advance him cash on the basis of his account balances. But his most audacious crime occurred when he obtained a Pan Am uniform and fake employee ID card to pose as a pilot. It is estimated that between the ages of 16 and 18, Abagnale travelled about 1.6 million kilometres on over 250 flights. He was eventually captured and sentenced to 12 years' imprisonment, but was released early after he agreed to assist authorities with fraud investigations.

Abagnale's story inspired the film *Catch Me If You Can*, starring Leonardo DiCaprio

© Thinkstock

MAN STEALS EINSTEIN'S BRAIN

■ **When genius Albert Einstein died, he left some very specific instructions for his remains: they were to be cremated.** His plans had been well thought out as he didn't want his body to be studied or worshipped. Despite these well-laid plans, on 18 April 1955, Einstein's brain was stolen.

Taken by a pathologist called Thomas Harvey, the brain was divided into blocks before being distributed among other pathologists to be studied. Harvey later sought retrospective permission from Einstein's son for the study of his father's brain, which he was reluctantly given.

After years of study, it was decided that Einstein's brain was formatted differently to those of other males. Portions of the brain had been discovered to have a higher proportion of glial cells, which provide protection to the neurons in the brain

LUNATIC CROOKS CAUGHT IN THE ACT

■ **Crimes can be subtle, shocking, grand, terrible or even downright impressive.** But for every train robbery and gruesome murder there are some felonies that are harder to categorise. Uncover history's weirdest criminal capers and the loons who dreamed them up - then made them a reality. Some took gumption, others sheer stupidity; either way, the perpetrators ended up red faced and rumbled.

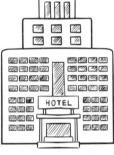

Man tries to cash billion-dollar cheque

Florida man Jeff Waters walked into a branch of Bank of America in 2015 and handed over a cheque for $368,000,000. It was from the US Bank of Idaho and had been issued in the 1990s. Waters said a homeless man had sold a blank cheque to him, telling him he could cash it for any amount.

Breaking, entering and ordering room service

Sometimes your hunger just wins out. That's what happened to Vinod Adhikary from Virginia when he broke into an Old Town Inn and decided to order some room service. Unsurprisingly, the hotel staff didn't expect a 2am order from an un-booked room and called it in.

The drug telemarketer

After deciding he wanted to get in on the lucrative yet illegal drug trade, one Florida-born teenager came up with a novel way to build a decent client base. Instead of hitting the streets, he starting cold calling numbers picked from the local phone book.

The Frankenstein pet

A woman in Warsaw, Poland was arrested following complaints from the neighbours about a smell in her home. Turns out she had killed over 100 cats and dogs and attempted to make a new breed of dog.

Attack of the condiments

In 2014, Japanese police arrested a man for the crime of squirting mayonnaise in the hair of a 15-year-old girl. It was revealed that it was a bit of a fetish for him; he'd been throwing handfuls of the condiment on random women in the street for months.

INVENTIONS & DISCOVERIES

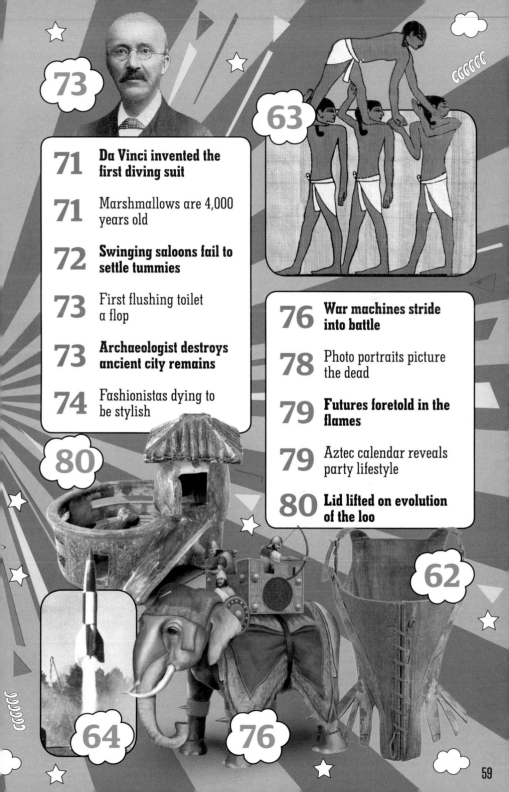

GAS-PROOF PRAM PROTECTS TODDLERS

■ **A mother walks her baby in a gas-resistant pram, designed by FW Mills in the years leading up to WWII.** The threat of gas attacks was imminent, and gas masks were distributed to everyone in Britain, including babies. This pram was an alternative, and had a lid with a glass panel and a gas filter on the top. An old motor horn bulb on the back expelled stale air and sucked in new.

AGE-OLD INTIMATES & UNDERGARMENTS EXPOSED

■ **From loincloths and corsets to codpieces and chastity belts, underwear solutions have varied significantly over time.** Take a peek at the fashions that have graced our nether regions over the centuries.

Thong Date unknown

Mentioning it may bring to mind modern women's underwear, but the thong actually has a history associated with masculinity. Like the loincloth, it was an early form of underwear, but it had a few perks that its counterpart couldn't provide. With a stretch of material to hold the genitals in place, it supported and protected active men. Sumo wrestlers wear a variant of the thong, known as the mawashi, and the thong's supportive capabilities inspired the creation of the jockstrap.

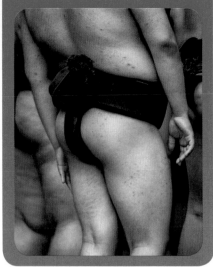

Corset 1300

Perhaps the most recognisable of all underwear, the corset's history is one that stretches back millennia, though it only really became the height of fashion in the 1600s. Bodices lined with whalebone and metal manipulated women's figures into fashionable shapes, with heaving breasts and waspish waists all the rage. The narrower the waist, the better – some dressmakers considered a 16-inch waist ideal, and achieving this would take about two years of training. Corsets posed plenty of health problems for their wearers, including bone fractures, bruised organs and a proneness to fainting.

Chastity belt 1896

First referred to in the early 15th century, the chastity belt may have been around for considerably longer. Cast in metal, they protected the virtues of the wearer from the perils of temptation and adultery. It's said that during the Crusades, chastity belts would safeguard women until their husbands' return. They really took off in the Victorian era, when physicians deemed masturbation to be the cause of insanity. They were – and are – available for both men and women.

Codpiece 14th century

The common codpiece was favoured by such nobles as King Henry VIII. Initially invented to cover the modesty of men in their open drawers, the codpiece's popularity surged thanks to its famous patron. As they evolved to emphasise the shape of men's genitals, Henry VIII stuffed his for a more well-endowed appearance. Little did many of his contemporaries realise he was also attempting to calm sores caused by syphilis with cool, wet cloths.

Drawers 1840s

Along with white weddings, Queen Victoria is thought to have inspired her nation to wear undergarments as a matter of norm. Variants on drawers had existed for centuries before, but it was only during Victoria's reign that they became an essential to every social class. Drawers often reached below the knees for both male and female wearers, and most people wore open drawers that featured a large opening in the crotch area, which facilitated bathroom-going and apparently kept the nether regions fresh and well ventilated.

Loincloth 1330 BCE

The most rudimentary form of underwear, and probably the most comfortable on this list, the loincloth harks back to the time of the Ancient Egyptians. Upon excavating his tomb, it was discovered that among many other treasures, Tutankhamun was buried with 145 loincloths – presumably to see him through his afterlife. King Tut wasn't the only one to cover his modesty; the Romans were also renowned for their loincloths. They could be worn as outer or underwear, mainly depending on the climate, but it's known that Ancient Egyptians wore theirs underneath kilt-like dress.

© Alamy; Getty Images

20,000 KILLED ON NAZI ROCKET PRODUCTION LINE

Who could have predicted that the Nazis' deadliest weapon would kill thousands of those tasked with building it? The V-2, short for Vergeltungswaffe-2 and also known as the A-4, was the world's first ballistic missile. Created by the Nazi military during World War II, the rocket was designed for sub-orbital space flight, meaning that upon reaching an altitude of around 80 kilometres (50 miles) it fell back to earth, exploding upon impact.

The V-2 programme is suggested to have been the single most expensive development project of the Third Reich. It claimed the lives of 20,000 inmates of the labour camp Mittelbau-Dora, who died constructing over 6,000 replicas of the device. It is thought to be the only weapon system of its kind to have caused more deaths during its production than in actual usage.

During its reign of limited service by the Nazis, over 3,000 clones were launched, resulting in the deaths of 7,250 civilians and military personnel. London received the second highest number of attacks, killing 2,752 civilians - statistically two people per rocket.

Improvements in accuracy increased greatly during its development, resulting in missiles claiming hundreds of lives at a time. Anti-aircraft and gunfire were no match for the V-2's speed and trajectory, dropping at four times the speed of sound. It is suggested that had the deployment of the V-2 rocket happened a few years earlier, Hilter might have won the war.

The V-2 was one of the Nazis' most destructive weapons

FIRST VENDING MACHINE FOR HOLY WATER

■ **It was Hero of Alexandria, a Greek engineer and mathematician who lived in the first century CE, who introduced the first vending machine.** For a small fee, you could purchase your very own holy water. A coin was placed into a slot where it fell onto a pan attached to a lever. The lever controlled a valve, allowing the holy water to flow. The weight of the coin caused the pan to tilt until the coin would slide off, and a counterweight restored the pan to its original position, cutting off the flow of water.

Cowry shells were legal tender in western Africa until the mid-19th century

SEASHELLS USED AS TRADING CURRENCY

■ **Shells have been used as currency by many different civilisations across the world.** The most commonly used pieces were the shells of small molluscs called cowry, which were particularly common in the Indian and Pacific oceans. The Chinese introduced cowry as a currency more than 3,000 years ago, and they were such an important aspect of their culture that the character for money is based on an image of a shell. Despite being difficult to counterfeit, when the natural supply of cowry in coastal regions ran low, people tried making imitation shells from other materials such as bones or horns.

ANCIENT SEISMOMETER PREDICTS QUAKES

■ **No, it's not a huge ornamental vase.** This earthquake detector was invented by the Chinese philosopher and astronomer Zhang Heng in 132 CE, during the Eastern Han Dynasty.

The 'Houfeng didong yi' as it was called, is described in the 5th-century *History of the Later Han Dynasty*, but an actual working version has not survived. This has led to much speculation about the details of how the pendulum mechanism would have worked inside the detector.

Heng built it on the principle that when winds are compressed into narrow spaces with no means of escape, they cause any obstacles to be dislodged and tossed "with a deep murmur." His device was claimed to be so sensitive it detected an earthquake 400 miles away, which was confirmed when a rider was dispatched to the area.

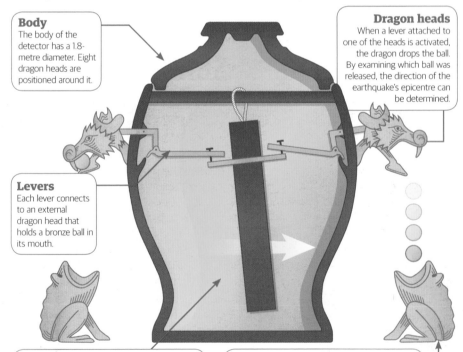

Body
The body of the detector has a 1.8-metre diameter. Eight dragon heads are positioned around it.

Dragon heads
When a lever attached to one of the heads is activated, the dragon drops the ball. By examining which ball was released, the direction of the earthquake's epicentre can be determined.

Levers
Each lever connects to an external dragon head that holds a bronze ball in its mouth.

Pendulum
The pendulum responds to earth tremors, swinging in the opposite direction to the tremor's epicentre and triggering one of the levers.

Toads
Eight toads are positioned beneath the dragon heads to catch dropped balls. When a toad catches a ball, it makes a sound to warn of the earthquake.

FAUX 'MISSING LINK' BONES FOOL SCIENTISTS

■ **The Piltdown Man was a famous hoax in which a species of extinct hominin was supposedly dug up at the Piltdown gravel pit in East Sussex, England, in 1912.** The excavation, led by scientist Charles Dawson, appeared to unearth the fossilised fragments of a cranium and jawbone that, on analysis by Dawson and some of his contemporaries, was confirmed as a new species: a missing link between apes and early humans.

For the next 40 years other scientists voiced serious doubts over the Piltdown Man's authenticity - especially as later genuine discoveries left the species isolated in the evolutionary sequence.

These misgivings were eventually proven justified in 1953 after an intensive re-examination of the bone fragments with modern scientific techniques revealed they were in fact from three different species. The cranium was that of a modern human, the jawbone from an orangutan and the teeth from a chimpanzee.

53-TON PLANE TAKES TO THE SKIES

◼ **Passengers and crew pose for a picture before boarding the German seaplane Dornier DO X on the day it carried 169 passengers above Lake Constance on the Rhine.** The plane had only been completed in June of that year and was the heaviest plane in the world, weighing 53 tons. Production ceased in the mid-Thirties after a series of accidents.

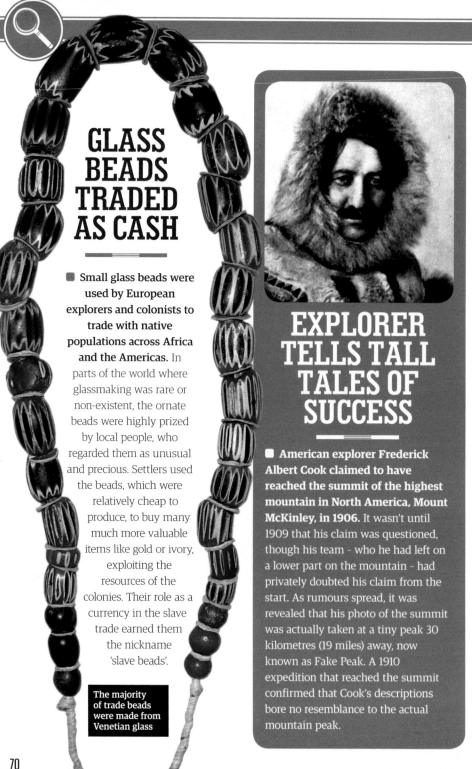

GLASS BEADS TRADED AS CASH

■ **Small glass beads were used by European explorers and colonists to trade with native populations across Africa and the Americas.** In parts of the world where glassmaking was rare or non-existent, the ornate beads were highly prized by local people, who regarded them as unusual and precious. Settlers used the beads, which were relatively cheap to produce, to buy many much more valuable items like gold or ivory, exploiting the resources of the colonies. Their role as a currency in the slave trade earned them the nickname 'slave beads'.

The majority of trade beads were made from Venetian glass

EXPLORER TELLS TALL TALES OF SUCCESS

■ **American explorer Frederick Albert Cook claimed to have reached the summit of the highest mountain in North America, Mount McKinley, in 1906.** It wasn't until 1909 that his claim was questioned, though his team – who he had left on a lower part on the mountain – had privately doubted his claim from the start. As rumours spread, it was revealed that his photo of the summit was actually taken at a tiny peak 30 kilometres (19 miles) away, now known as Fake Peak. A 1910 expedition that reached the summit confirmed that Cook's descriptions bore no resemblance to the actual mountain peak.

DA VINCI INVENTED THE FIRST DIVING SUIT

■ **In 1499, while living in Venice, a city famous for its network of waterways, da Vinci conceived a way for a human to breathe underwater.** His diving suit was made out of pigskin leather and featured cane tubes connected to a floating bell, through which the wearer would be able to breathe. Da Vinci was once again light years ahead of his time, and it would be centuries before his suit would be studied again and further developed to what we would now call scuba equipment.

Another one of his concepts, the use of a leather pouch to keep air underwater for breathing, formed the basis of what would become an early version of the aqualung in the 19th century.

Da Vinci's design has been tested and proved to have worked

MARSHMALLOWS ARE 4,000 YEARS OLD

■ **The popular campfire treat has a more detailed history than you may think.** The earliest marshmallows date back to as early as 2,000 BCE when the Ancient Egyptians served them as a delicacy. They were made from the sap of the mallow plant and mixed with nuts and honey. The sweets first appeared in their current form in the 19th century when French candy makers mixed the initial ingredients with egg whites and sugar.

Gimbals
The cabin was suspended from the Bessemer's main deck by a series of pivoted supports called gimbals.

Cabin
The main cabin was 21m (70ft) long, 9.1m (30ft) wide and 6.1m (20ft) high.

Hydraulics
The position of the floor was dictated by a series of hydraulic cylinders.

SWINGING SALOONS FAIL TO SETTLE TUMMIES

■ **The SS Bessemer was an experimental Victorian ship that attempted to solve the age-old problem of passenger seasickness.** The idea was that if the main saloon could remain stationary (horizontal) in relation to the tilting hull of the ship, then passengers would not be exposed to stomach-churning movements while on board.

The cabin was isolated by suspending it on gimbals from the deck and kept horizontal mechanically by an array of hydraulic cylinders controlled by a steersman. To keep the cabin floor at 180 degrees, the steersman simply consulted a

spirit level to determine the tilt and then counteracted it. On paper it seemed like an ingenious solution; in reality, it proved a monumental failure.

While the suspension system worked, mitigating a large amount of cabin sway, the shifting centre of gravity made the ship almost unsteerable and very unpredictable while at sea - two factors that led it to crash into Calais Pier on its first trip. The poor performance at sea, catastrophic maiden voyage and huge costs involved in the project saw it being wound up. The ship was dismantled only four years after its first - and last - commercial voyage.

FLUSHING TOILET A FLOP

■ **Contrary to popular belief, the inventor of the flushing toilet was not Thomas Crapper.** It was actually a member of Queen Elizabeth I's court, Sir John Harrington.

First described in 1596, Harrington's device was composed of a deep oval bowl, which was made waterproof with a mixture of pitch, resin and wax. This was flushed with water released from a cistern above the toilet.

In spite of this breakthrough, it took more than 200 years for the flushing toilet to catch on. Advances in technology that accompanied the Industrial Revolution helped to spur on the toilet's development, as did the invention of the 'S-trap' in 1775. Still present in modern toilets, this S-shaped pipe allows standing water to seal off the bowl, preventing gases from the sewer escaping into your bathroom.

ARCHAEOLOGIST DESTROYS ANCIENT CITY REMAINS

■ **Historical landmarks like the pyramids of Giza and Stonehenge have been preserved for thousands of years, but there are many more that been destroyed and lost forever.** Perhaps one of the biggest losses of all time was the work of the archaeologist who set out to find it. Heinrich Schliemann was determined to uncover the ancient city of Troy. In 1871, he began excavations where he believed Troy was located and quickly made his way through the upper levels, believing that the historical city lay at the lowest level of the stacked cities he discovered. Schliemann used various methods and even used dynamite to flatten city walls. In fact, the level Schliemann sought was built several thousand years too early. It is believed that his team ploughed through and destroyed the ancient city.

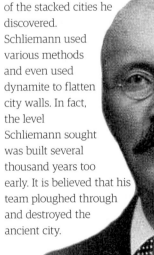

FASHIONISTAS DYING TO BE STYLISH

■ **Some people will do whatever it takes to look good.** But what if your beauty hacks left you bloody, bruised or breathless? Here are some of the craziest contraptions that people suffered for style.

CRÈME SCIENTIFIQUE

CURATIVE EMBELLISSANTE

THO-RADIA

Radioactive skin cream

In their quest for a face with that youthful healthy 'glow', the women of the 20th century began smothering their faces in radioactive creams. For a fresh-faced, radiant complexion, many women of the interwar period turned to lotions that were made with radium – so radioactive it glows in the dark. Of all the sellers of radioactive creams, a French brand named Tho-Radia topped the charts with their radium-thorium recipe. With their range of creams, toothpastes and cosmetics, women applied radioactive makeup on a daily basis. As you'd expect, radiation poisoning and cancer figures soared.

Corsets

The fatal finery of choice in the 19th century, corsets already had a bad reputation in the 1800s, with doctors frowning upon them and a plethora of literature condemning the undergarment. In 1848, one doctor even suggested that wearing a corset was akin to committing suicide. To achieve the hourglass figure so popular at the time, women's corsets would be laced as tightly as possible, with the recommended waist size set to 18 inches.

Wearing their corsets, ladies often experienced headaches, breathing trouble and fainting. That was just the tip of the iceberg, however – there were widespread reports of broken ribs, and extreme lacing led to displaced internal organs, deformed rib cages and even death.

Foot binding

This was a trend that took China by storm for more than a millennium. Popular during the Song dynasty (10th-13th century), women with small feet were considered the height of elegance. To achieve the look, the foot binding process began early – between the ages of two and seven – while their feet were supple and soft, and they were blissfully unaware of the pain they were about to experience. First, all but their big toes would be broken and folded down into the ball of the foot. Next, the arch would be bent to its extreme, then the foot would be bound in the tightest cloth. From here, years of tight binding would ensure that the foot didn't grow to an unsightly size. The cruel practice would cut off circulation in the toes, which more often than not led to infection and gangrene. Feet would be covered in sores and often gave off a foul stench – all the better that they covered up with elegant little silk shoes, then.

Tapeworm diet

Feeling fat, but not willing to exercise or embrace a healthier diet? Tapeworms are sure to solve the problem. In the early 20th century, tapeworms and tapeworm eggs were sold in jars and as pills as a form of dieting option. Simply consume your tapeworms, wait for them to absorb your food, then – once you're down to your ideal weight – take an anti-parasitic tablet. Results were guaranteed with the tapeworm diet, but it came with a host of terrible side-effects, including cysts in the brain, spinal cord and eyes, meningitis and epilepsy. Maybe stick to the celery sticks...

The deadly nightshade drops caused the user's eyes to dilate

Deadly nightshade eye drops

Sickly sweet and toxic to the touch, deadly nightshade could be found in most Roman women's beauty regimes. Also known as belladonna ('beautiful woman' in Italian), the poisonous plant was distilled into eye drops that gave the user that classic, sexy doe-eyed look. Too strong a mix, however, and they would go blind. Accidentally ingest some, and they could expect extreme hallucinations, brain damage and death.

© Alamy; Getty Images

WAR MACHINES STRIDE INTO BATTLE

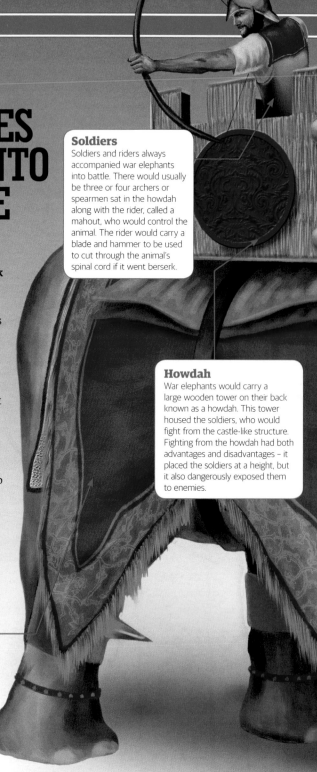

■ **When you think of military vehicles, we bet you don't think of these four-legged gentle giants.** Are we right? But the Persians did indeed put elephants to such a task in the 4th century BCE. Collossal in size, these war tanks were an intimidating presence on the battlefront, elevating warriors to a height that gave them a distinct advantage against their opponents. The drawbacks? Vehicle maintenance would have been a pain, with feeding, watering and cleaning up after the elephants likely to have been a mammoth task.

Soldiers

Soldiers and riders always accompanied war elephants into battle. There would usually be three or four archers or spearmen sat in the howdah along with the rider, called a mahout, who would control the animal. The rider would carry a blade and hammer to be used to cut through the animal's spinal cord if it went berserk.

Howdah

War elephants would carry a large wooden tower on their back known as a howdah. This tower housed the soldiers, who would fight from the castle-like structure. Fighting from the howdah had both advantages and disadvantages – it placed the soldiers at a height, but it also dangerously exposed them to enemies.

Gender

War elephants used in battles were exclusively male. It is commonly believed that this is because they were faster and more aggressive, but this is incorrect. Males were more suitable as any females in battle would flee from males – a very unreliable and dangerous trait on the battlefield. Instead, female elephants were used for logistics work and transportation.

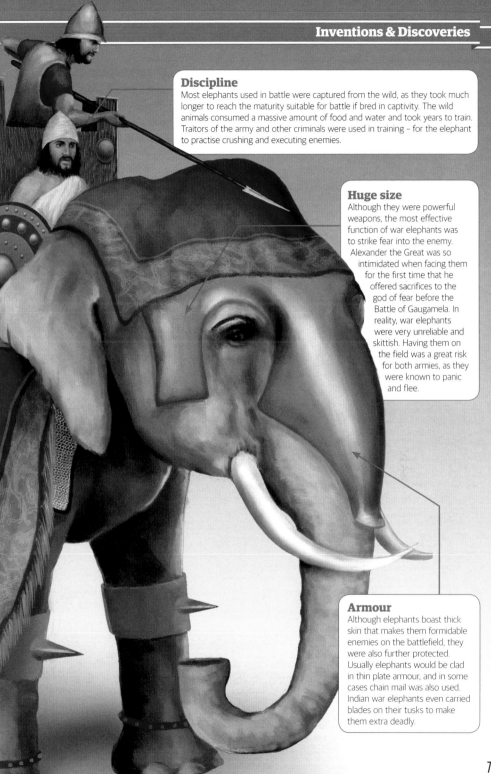

Discipline

Most elephants used in battle were captured from the wild, as they took much longer to reach the maturity suitable for battle if bred in captivity. The wild animals consumed a massive amount of food and water and took years to train. Traitors of the army and other criminals were used in training – for the elephant to practise crushing and executing enemies.

Huge size

Although they were powerful weapons, the most effective function of war elephants was to strike fear into the enemy. Alexander the Great was so intimidated when facing them for the first time that he offered sacrifices to the god of fear before the Battle of Gaugamela. In reality, war elephants were very unreliable and skittish. Having them on the field was a great risk for both armies, as they were known to panic and flee.

Armour

Although elephants boast thick skin that makes them formidable enemies on the battlefield, they were also further protected. Usually elephants would be clad in thin plate armour, and in some cases chain mail was also used. Indian war elephants even carried blades on their tusks to make them extra deadly.

PHOTO PORTRAITS PICTURE THE DEAD

In the days before modern medicine, death was a common part of everyday life. From the time of the Protestant Reformation, painted portraits of the dead were displayed in homes as a way to remember the deceased. But with the dawn of photography, mourning portraits took a morbid turn. The introduction of the daguerreotype in 1839 meant that portraiture became much more popular as many people could afford to pay a photographer to capture their likeness. But in a world where mortality rates were high and photography was new, post-mortem portraits were often the only chance people had of capturing their prematurely departed loved one. Corpses were often made to look like they were caught mid-sleep or were propped up with their eyes open to appear more lifelike.

© Thinkstock; Top Foto

AZTEC CALENDAR REVEALS PARTY LIFESTYLE

■ **The Ancient Aztecs of Mexico didn't do things by half, and that includes the means by which the civilisation measured time.** The system was incredibly complex, comprising a triple calendar that marked a long list of religious festivals and gave each day a unique name and number.

The three wheels were used to measure different facets of time: 'Tonalpohualli' represented a 260-day long year, which was broken down into periods of 20 days. Each of these 20 days also had its own symbol and name. The second calendar, 'Xiuhpohualli', was used to record years and was based on a 365-day solar cycle – again, these were broken down into 18 groups of 20 days, with each group attributed a religious festival. The third was known as the 'calendar round' and bound the other two together.

FUTURES FORETOLD IN THE FLAMES

■ **In Ancient China, the discipline of divination – interpreting the future through omens or signs – was all the rage.** One form in particular, pyromancy, was perhaps the most popular. The practice of reading signs from the flames had spread across the globe and its presence in China included the use of words inscribed in bone. Normally the scapula (shoulder bone) of an ox or plastrons (the flat underside of a turtle's shell) were used, with pilgrims advised to carve a question regarding a request for blessing or good fortune from the gods on the bones. A metal rod heated in a fire would then be inserted into the shell until it cracked, with the diviner reading these fragments, or 'oracle bones', to interpret a celestial response.

© Alamy

LID LIFTED ON EVOLUTION OF THE LOO

■ **Where did our ancestors go to spend a penny?** And how long did it take for rudimentary loos to develop into the all-singing, all dancing flushing toilets in use today? It may not be the most significant part of everyday life, but these toilets offer an insight into how comfort breaks were taken throughout the centuries.

Roman latrina
c. 200 BCE

Located at the rear of Roman forts, these communal toilet spaces were nowhere near as private as today's restrooms. Soldiers would sit side-by-side and chat about the issues of the day. Then, when they had done their business, instead of using toilet paper, a sponge on a stick was used to clean the bottoms of every soldier. Away from the military, toilets tended to be in a slightly better condition and comfort rooms in the city could even have their own plumbing, using water from the local bathhouse to wash away the waste.

The Ostia Antica site has some of the best preserved Roman toilets

Dry earth closet
1859

First developed by Henry Moule, the dry earth closet was an alternative to the water closet and the cesspit. A few decades later, a patent was taken on with the design for a mechanical earth closet that had a system to turn the manure into compost, lessening both the smell and the waste product. This was done by putting dry earth into a container at the top of the loo, which would fall into the bowl and decay the waste as quickly as possible. Modern versions of the dry earth closet are still used today and go by the term 'composting toilet'.

Pig toilet c. 9 CE

A pig toilet is a simple type of dry toilet, consisting of an outhouse mounted over a pigsty and connected via a chute. After doing one's business, the feces falls down the chute and is consumed by the pigs below. This type of loo was common in Han Dynasty China, and can still be found in India and South Korea. People in Ancient China were often buried with funerary models of pig toilets; placing symbols of everything from food and weapons to toilets within tombs ensured their provision in the afterlife.

Pissoir 1830

The first modern public urinals were developed in France and installed on the major boulevards of Paris. They were initially more famous for their use as barricades during the 1830 July Revolutions, but soon enough the pissoir, or *vespasienne*, become a staple on the streets of Europe's cities and has been in high demand since the Industrial Revolution's mass migration to urban areas. They have reduced the incidence of public urination, and as some public toilets charge for use, they provided a source of income for the state – and so the origin of the euphemism 'spend a penny'.

Japan leads the way in modern toilet design. This washlet is an electronic bidet

Electronic loo 1982

For some, the flushing toilet just isn't enough, and electronic toilets cater for those looking for a more indulgent loo experience. Japan in particular has taken to these bidet toilet seats, which are the result of the influx of western toilets into Japanese society. They are designed to clean your bits after you've finished your business, issuing a jet of warm water and a drier for your bottom. Other modern contraptions include water-saving measures, seat warmers, built-in fragrances and relaxation music. Some toilets even tell you the health of your waste.

© Alamy: DK Images

HEALTH & MEDICINE

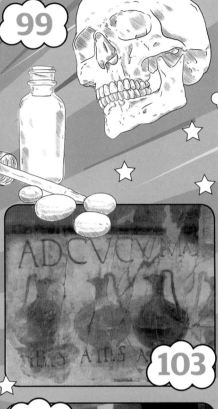

CRAZY CONTRAPTIONS USED BY DOCTORS

Healing hands have, through time, been as much a doctor's requirement as a sturdy stomach. As technology has advanced, so too have the medical tools and machines at a healer's disposal. Which means that what we now consider to be time-tested treatments were once high-risk endeavours. Then there's the procedures the preceded them. These curious contraptions are enough to instil fear in the hardiest mind, but they were often the best route to survival.

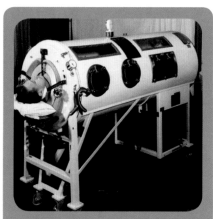

Iron lung
1928, USA

These were among the first life-support machines, gaining fame for saving polio victims whose breathing muscles had been paralysed by the disease. The devices consisted of an airtight chamber connected to an air pump. They worked by sucking air in and out of the chamber, causing the patient's lungs to contract and expand, in turn allowing them to breathe. Many polio patients recovered after spending only minutes inside an iron lung, while others were less fortunate. Those who didn't enjoy a quick recovery spent their entire lives looking at the world through a mirror attached to the top of the machine.

Lithotome
1780, Britain

What may look like an instrument of torture, this device was well-meaning but painful nonetheless. This long, claw-like instrument was inserted up the urethra and into the bladder. The surgeon would then use it to grip onto small bladder stones and pull them out, or use the blade in order to slice up the larger ones so that the patient would be able to pass them naturally. The entire procedure would have been carried out while the patient was wide awake – and undoubtedly suffering a significant amount of pain! The surgeon also had to make sure they didn't slice the bladder in the process, which could lead the patient to bleed to death.

This 18th-century lithotome had a spring-loaded, mahogany handle

Bullet extractor

16th century, Europe

The introduction of firearms to the battlefield in the early-13th century completely changed the face of warfare. Until the invention of this revolutionary device, only bullets that resided close to the surface of the skin could be removed. But this bullet extractor allowed surgeons to dig much deeper, in search of more probing bullets. The device consisted of a hollow rod containing a screw, which could be lengthened or shortened using the handle at the top. The instrument would be placed inside the patient's wound and the screw lengthened in order to pierce the bullet and remove it.

> This 16th-century bullet extractor was made of steel and had ornate handles

Reduction device

5th century BCE, Greece

Hippocrates is considered the father of Western medicine, and he detailed the oldest known method for treating a dislocated shoulder. He developed a ladder-like device, across which the injured arm was slung and then pulled downward with significant force. In the 16th century, French royal surgeon Ambroise Paré reintroduced Hippocrates' method, and it is still used today.

Osteotome

1830, Germany

In the days before general anaesthetics, amputations would have been incredibly painful and incredibly dangerous procedures. Bones were often splintered and the tissue around them damaged by the harsh impact of a hammer and chisel or the jolts of a saw. Surgeons needed to find a way to speed up the procedure and reduce the risk of complications. The solution came in the form of the osteotome – a device with a chain and sharp cutting teeth that was cranked manually. What this device was, in fact, was the first-ever chainsaw.

MEDIEVAL BARBERS MOONLIGHTED AS DENTISTS

Barbers were pretty versatile in the Middle Ages. As well as being handy with the hairdressing scissors, they could also carry out blood letting, tooth extractions, enemas and surgical procedures.

French surgeon Guy de Chauliac in his 1363 surgical treatise Le Grande Chirurgie advised on preventing at all costs the removal of teeth. He recommended the use of mouthwashes, gargles, masticatories, ointments, rubbings, cauterisations, fumigations, fillings and filings to keep the mouth healthy. But Chauliac's expert advice was not the general rule.

There were hundreds of folk remedies for toothache, from poultices and herbal mixtures to charms, astrology and amulets. When all else failed you could visit the barber or pray. Even the English physician, John of Gaddesden, in his 1314 work Rosa Anglica, suggests that toothache can be cured if you pray on 9 February, the feast day of St Apollonia (who was burned alive after having all her teeth knocked out back in 249 CE).

It was not until the 18th century that the business of the two professions would be totally separated in England and France.

'BLESS YOU' ISSUED AS A PLAGUE DETERRENT

■ **The action of wishing someone well after a sneeze stretches back thousands of years, so it's difficult to pin one explanation down.** However, the phrase 'God bless you' after a sneeze can be attributed to Pope Gregory I in 590. During this time an outbreak of bubonic plague was raging in the Eastern Roman Empire. In response, the Pope ordered a series of endless prayers, as sneezing was regarded as a sign of the disease. 'God bless you' was seen as a method to prevent the sneezer from contracting the plague.

LOVE AFFAIR ENDS IN CASTRATION

■ **Few relationships have ended as badly as that of Heloise and Abelard.** Heloise was a gifted student whose ambition in life was to understand human existence, so her uncle Fulbert, the canon of Notre Dame, enlisted the help of Peter Abelard, a renowned philosopher some 20 years her senior.

Despite the age gap, the pair fell in love - then pregnant. Fearing an imminent scandal, they fled to Brittany and married in an attempt to appease Heloise's furious uncle. But it wasn't enough. While Heloise sought refuge in a convent, Fulbert ordered his men to attack Abelard in one of the most humiliating ways possible: castration.

The pair escaped with their lives by taking holy orders as a nun and a monk. They were separated for years, but wrote to each other occasionally. Seven letters exist today, featuring remorse, sadness, pain and anger. Abelard told Heloise he never really loved her, while Heloise told Abelard she never wanted to be his wife. While their tragic story has lived on, their love for each other did not.

© Thinkstock

URINE & LIVE HENS USED AS BLACK DEATH CURES

■ **Killing up to 200 million across Europe, Black Death struck fear in the minds of 14th century men and women.** In desperation, a number of herbal treatments were harnessed to target the disease.

Sufferers were regularly prescribed solutions of ground emeralds or potions made from the crushed shells of newly laid eggs mixed with chopped marigolds, ale and treacle. Treacle was a leading remedy, though it had to be at least ten years old to have any potency. Another effective curative was urine; two glasses a day were widely thought to fend off disease.

Treatment of buboes was a trickier affair. People believed they could draw out pestilence by holding bread against the boils and burying it - or, more incredibly, by strapping a live hen to the swelling. Physicians later discovered that lancing buboes, draining the pus and applying poultices was relatively effective in the early stages. Such poultices usually consisted of tree resin, white lily root and then dried human excrement, arsenic or dried toad.

Since the Black Death was allegedly miasmatic, the best preventative was thought to be carrying pouches of sweet herbs and spices (or balls of perfume called pomanders), and burning them in your home. But many people fasted, prayed and joined the Flagellants in order to pay penance for their sins. The last resort? Kill suspected witches or well-poisoners, and wait for Saturn to move out of the House of Jupiter.

Uniform of a plague doctor from the early-1600s

PROSTHETIC LIMBS LET US WALK LIKE EGYPTIANS

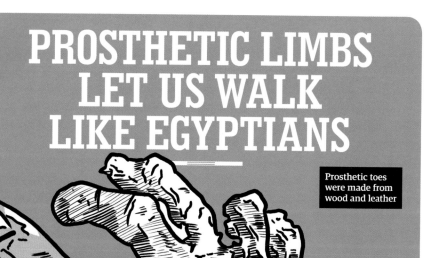

Prosthetic toes were made from wood and leather

■ **The Ancient Egyptians have been credited with the invention of many things we continue to use today, from the ox-drawn plough to the written language.** They are also believed to have made the first prosthetic limbs. Many fake body parts have been discovered over the years, buried alongside Egyptian mummies, including feet, noses and even penises.

At first it was thought that these were purely symbolic, ensuring that the dead could procreate, run from danger or smell sweet wines in the afterlife. However, in 2000, an artificial wood-and-leather toe dating from between 950 and 710 BCE was unearthed. It was later found to be functional after it was tested out on volunteers. The discovery demonstrates just how resourceful this civilisation really was, and how little the designs changed over the millennia.

TUDOR DOCTORS' TOOLS OF TERROR

Lancet

A core tool of the phlebotomist, lancets were small triangular blades that featured a groove to channel spilled blood. They would be inserted into key points around the patient's body depending on their particular imbalance of humours and astrological readings, and would drain away a healthy amount of blood.

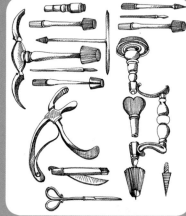

Scarifactor

A precise, painful-looking piece of equipment, the scarifactor was a multiplication of the lancet blade. Tiny slices of metal sit in rows and enable the blood-letter to speed up their work, quickly carving out exact measures of blood taken from light surface wounds across the patient's whole body.

Trepan

Used to bore holes into the skull, the trepan was essentially a bone-grinding corkscrew. At the time, most illnesses of the head were thought to be curable by exposing its insides to a little more fresh air. From migraines and epileptic fits to symptoms of ADHD – there's nothing a bit of trepanning couldn't fix.

Healers thought they could cure illness by releasing blood

Knife

Ranging from tiny scalpels to great meat carvers, barber-surgeons had a wide array of knives at their disposal, so they could choose the perfect tool to suit their patients' ailments. Depending on the hygiene standards of the surgeon in question, you could live or die depending on the cleanliness of the blade – more often than not, they'd simply be rinsed in cold water in between uses.

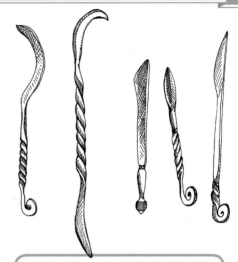

Other names for this device included flem, flew, flue, fleame and phleam

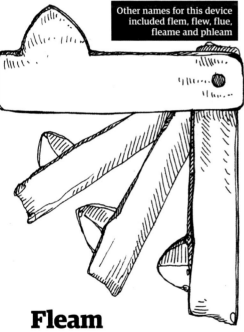

Cautery iron

When amputations needed to be made, barber-surgeons used a great circular knife that could whip all the meat off a bone in one stroke, followed by a heavy saw in as few seconds as possible. They would then seal the wound by stretching pig skin across it and using a hot cautery iron to burn everything shut. No anaesthetics beyond alcohol, mind.

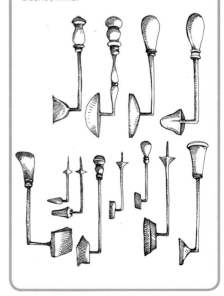

Fleam

In a similar vein to the lancet, the fleam consisted of a small triangular blade that was designed to puncture veins. This instrument was made to be as fast, accurate and painless as was physically possible. It came with a special fleam stick, and if you tapped the tool with the stick, then the attached blade would instantly pierce the skin. Not pain-free, but close enough.

THE WOMEN WHO HAD 'WANDERING WOMBS'

■ **'Hysteria' was a common diagnosis during the Victorian period.** According to one physician in 1859, it affected a quarter of all women. Symptoms ranged wildly, from fainting, anxiety, irritability, increase in sexual desire and loss of sexual desire, to increased and decreased appetite, cramps, and, according to historian Rachel Maines, "a tendency to cause trouble." While Ancient Greeks believed the condition was the result of a 'wandering womb', or the retention of poisonous female semen not released through regular intercourse, the Victorians simply believed it to be a 'women's issue', often treating it through cold, high-pressure showers or, in particularly extreme cases, forcibly admitting women into asylums for hysterectomies. Today we know its causes range from premenstrual cramps and anxiety through to epilepsy and more serious mental health issues.

30-SECOND AMPUTATION DOCTOR

■ **In the 1800s, London doctor Robert Liston gained a reputation as a surgeon who could complete an amputation procedure in 30 seconds or less.** He was considered to be one of the finest surgeons in the country because of the speed he could have the horrifying operation completed in, helping to reduce the trauma the patient endured. However, speed often meant carelessness in the operation of the task.

In one now infamous incident, Liston was performing a leg amputation but in his haste to beat his best time, he sawed through the patient's testicles, then accidentally cut through an orderly's hand before finally stabbing a spectator in the stomach, causing him to bleed to death over the operating table. It was said to be the only surgery in history with a 300 per cent mortality rate.

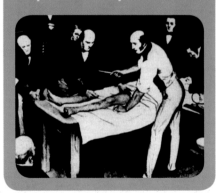

© Alamy

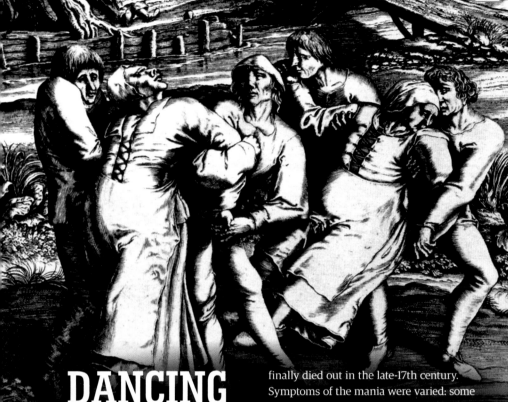

DANCING PLAGUE KILLS 400

■ **In 1518, dancing mania seized the city of Strasbourg, France (then part of the Holy Roman Empire).** For days and nights on end, the plague spread from person to person, causing them to dance until they dropped - literally. In all, around 400 people were infected with this fatal dancing fever.

This wasn't the first breakout of the plague - it struck a nearby town in the 14th century, while the late-16th century saw smaller outbreaks across Europe. It finally died out in the late-17th century. Symptoms of the mania were varied: some claimed outbreaks were spontaneous, while others justified them as organised events. However, contemporary sources claimed the dancers were unconscious and had no control over their bodies. For some, dancing would lead to ecstasy and fulfilment, but for many, dancers suffered hallucinations, fits, convulsions, broken bones and, ultimately, death.

In the 1518 outbreak, both supernatural and astrological causes were ruled out, so it was simply agreed that the best way to combat the plague was to encourage more dancing. Musicians were hired, and venues and stages were set up.

But what was it that caused an entire town to dance to their deaths? Many blame ergot poisoning, but others theorised that the event was staged by cult

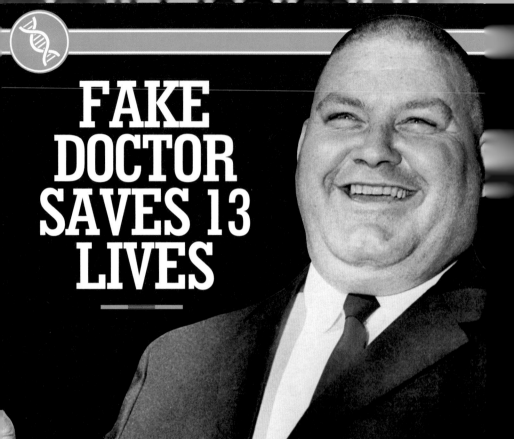

FAKE DOCTOR SAVES 13 LIVES

■ **To those who met him, Ferdinand Waldo Demara seemed to have impressive credentials.** At various points in his life he was a surgeon, teacher, Navy officer, assistant prison warden, hospital orderly, lawyer, editor and a cancer researcher. He also had stints as a Trappist and Benedictine monk. To land these roles he made up his identity according to whatever situation he put himself in, often borrowing the personas of living people.

Demara would forge transcripts and documents in order to successfully impersonate others, earning him the nickname 'the Great Impostor'. He managed to excel and evade capture in most of the jobs he secured, and those who knew him would remark on his high IQ and photographic memory.

But his most audacious deception would prove to be his undoing. During the Korean War he assumed the identity of Canadian doctor Joseph Cyr, and in 1951 he worked on the destroyer Cayuga for several months. He performed surgery on soldiers with the aid of a medical textbook, even going as far as extracting a bullet from a man's chest in a major operation.

Demara saved 13 lives and was hailed a hero, but subsequent press coverage unmasked him as an impostor. His story was so mind-boggling that he himself would be impersonated by actor Tony Curtis in the film *The Great Impostor*.

HYGIENE HABITS THREATEN HEALTH

■ **Plenty of gruesome practices were once considered healthy that we wouldn't touch today.** Now science is there to prove the importance of cleanliness and good personal hygiene, but past societies were nonplussed about the measures required to keep themselves fit and healthy. These cringe worthy examples will make you grateful you were born in the modern age.

Urine mouthwash

Ammonia, a common ingredient of household cleaners, is also found in urine. When the Romans got wind of these cleaning properties, they used their waste to clean their clothes. However, they also believed its stain removing powers could clean and whiten teeth, so they regularly gargled with it as mouthwash.

Toilet closets

In Medieval houses, toilets were basically a bowl covered by a slab of wood with a hole in the middle. They could usually be found in closets called garderobes, and people would often keep their clothes in there as the smell helped to keep moths away.

Mouse-skin eyebrows

Beauty fashions have fluctuated through the ages, and during the 18th century it was considered unattractive for women to have thick eyebrows. Instead they kept them plucked thin and pencilled in a high arch, or they shaved off their eyebrows and replaced them with false eyebrows made from mouse skin.

Rotten teeth

The Tudors knew that sugar rotted their teeth, but because sugar was so expensive and therefore a sign of wealth, Tudor women would deliberately blacken their teeth to make them look rotten.

Hair-raising treatments

A common treatment for baldness in the 17th century was to mix potassium salts with chicken droppings and rub it into the scalp. Alternatively, one method for removing hair involved creating a paste from eggs, vinegar and cat dung.

© Thinkstock

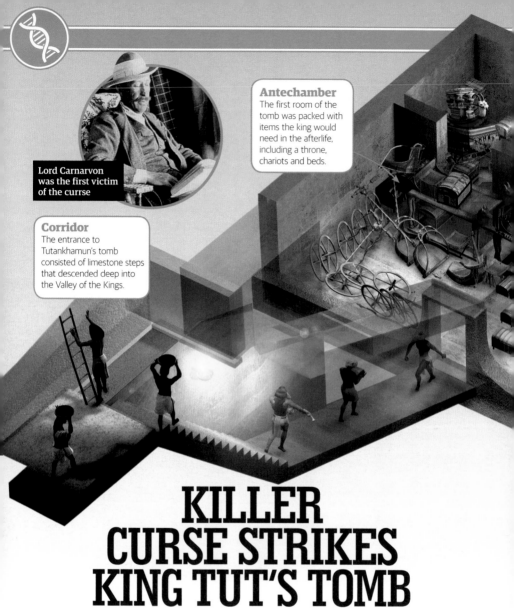

Lord Carnarvon was the first victim of the currse

Antechamber
The first room of the tomb was packed with items the king would need in the afterlife, including a throne, chariots and beds.

Corridor
The entrance to Tutankhamun's tomb consisted of limestone steps that descended deep into the Valley of the Kings.

Lord Carnarvon was the first victim of the currse

KILLER CURSE STRIKES KING TUT'S TOMB

■ **When renowned Egyptologist Howard Carter unlocked the tomb of the boy king, he unleashed a mysterious curse...** At least that's how the legend goes.

The tomb was opened in 1922, and soon followed the demise of a number of those involved in this momentous event. The media was whipped up into a frenzy. The first victim was Lord Carnarvon, the man who had sponsored the search; he passed away just a few months later. He died from a mosquito bite that had become infected after he caught it shaving.

Ten more people met unfortunate and mysterious ends shortly after, and each was attributed to the killer curse.

Annex
The smallest room contained items like oil, wine, food, pottery and baskets. It had been burgled several times.

Burial chamber
This is where the pharaoh's sarcophagus was found, containing his mummy, his solid-gold coffin, and his famous death mask.

Treasure chamber
Some of the most valuable treasures were found in this room, including a gilded shrine that contained Tutankhamun's canopic jars.

© Thinkstock

97

LIFE-SAVING DRUG DISCOVERED BY ACCIDENT

■ **The development of penicillin is an amazing story of accidental discovery.** Working hard in his laboratory for months on end, Scottish scientist Alexander Fleming decided to take a month-long holiday in August 1928 to see his family.

Quickly throwing some of his things together, he promptly left London, leaving his workplace in a bit of a mess. Among the mess were a number of Petri dishes filled with the bacteria staphylococci. Little did Fleming realise, these Petri dishes would help him revolutionise the world of medicine with a huge discovery.

On returning to London and entering his laboratory, Fleming immediately noticed that a distinctive mould had grown on one of the Petri dishes. In doing so it had killed all of the nearby staphylococci bacteria.

After tidying up, Fleming attempted to regrow the mould himself in a pure culture. He succeeded shortly after and, after trialling the culture on various bacteria, he saw that it successfully destroyed several that caused disease. Realising what he had discovered, Fleming published his findings and the precursor to the modern-day antibiotic was born.

WORLD'S WACKIEST REMEDIES REVEALED

Through history, humanity has sought remedies for every ailment under the Sun. Based on nothing but speculation, the oddest practices you could possibly imagine were adopted in the hope of achieving relief for the patient. Plenty of such treatments were more than a little uncomfortable (not to mention unsuccessful) - they were mad, dangerous and often fatal. But desperate times called for desperate measures. Take a look at some of history's most innovative and insane remedies and thank heaven medicine has advanced so much.

Sleep with a skull
In Ancient Babylon, a skull was thought to cure plenty of ailments. Depending on the problem, patients would be told to sleep next to a skull for weeks at a time, or to perform a kissing and licking ritual on the skull.

Mercury for STDs
For those nasty cases of syphilis, mercury was a popular cure. It often worked, but patients would find themselves suffering from a host of new symptoms, including tremors, muscle spasms and even hallucinations.

Trepanning
This popular treatment was used to remedy headaches and brain problems. However, the act of drilling holes into the skull was usually performed without any kind of pain relief or anaesthetic.

Bloodletting
To balance out the four humours (yellow bile, black bile, phlegm and blood), bloodletting was popular for combatting illness for thousands of years. But lose too much blood and you'd end up losing your life.

Goat testicles
In the early 20th century, one faux-doctor claimed that he could cure impotence by surgically implanting the testicles of a goat in a man's scrotum. It's safe to say this didn't work.

CURES THAT WERE (LITERALLY) MAN-MADE

Today cannibalism is considered somewhat of a social faux-pas, a one-way ticket to a psychiatric ward. However, up until only three centuries ago there was a slight loophole to this. The consumption of human bones and blood was considered a medical cure for various ailments, from headaches to epilepsy.

One of the most popular remedies was Mummy Powder, which was used to cure ulcers, stomachaches and headaches. This all-round cure was supposedly made from

the ground-up remains of Ancient Egyptian pharaohs, though it's more likely that practitioners would grind up the remains of locals from nearby graveyards.

Charles II was a keen follower of corpse medicine and made popular the King's Drops, which was a liquid elixir made from powdered skull. He'd regularly take his drops to promote general all-round health.

However, it wasn't just the royals and aristocracy that believed they could benefit from corpse medicine. King's blood was considered to be a cure for many ailments that peasants suffered from. When Charles I was executed, crowds surged forward to mop up the regal blood from the streets. Similarly, the Romans thought gladiators' blood was a cure for epilepsy.

Some of the longest enduring corpse medicines were ointments made up of human fat. These ointments were said to help with joint pain, arthritis and muscle cramps. The fat of the dead was mixed with alcoholic drinks and consumed. It's thought that this practice lasted well into the 1920s in Holland.

Charles I's execution. Royal blood was considered curative

KET HAVS

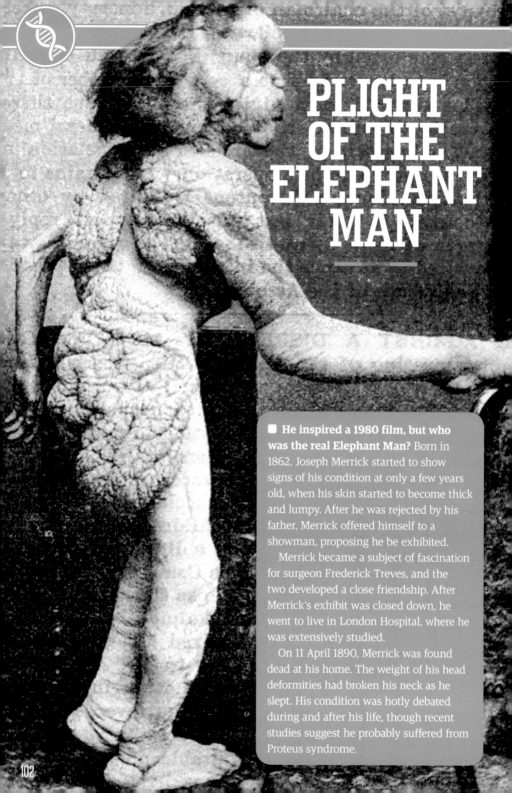

PLIGHT OF THE ELEPHANT MAN

■ **He inspired a 1980 film, but who was the real Elephant Man?** Born in 1862, Joseph Merrick started to show signs of his condition at only a few years old, when his skin started to become thick and lumpy. After he was rejected by his father, Merrick offered himself to a showman, proposing he be exhibited.

Merrick became a subject of fascination for surgeon Frederick Treves, and the two developed a close friendship. After Merrick's exhibit was closed down, he went to live in London Hospital, where he was extensively studied.

On 11 April 1890, Merrick was found dead at his home. The weight of his head deformities had broken his neck as he slept. His condition was hotly debated during and after his life, though recent studies suggest he probably suffered from Proteus syndrome.

NAPOLEON'S COUGH KILLS 1,200

■ More of an urban myth than a certified historical fact, the idea of the self-appointed French emperor Napoleon Bonaparte accidentally ordering the execution of 1,200 prisoners has nonetheless become the stuff of legend.

Rumour has it that the event occurred when Napoleon was considering whether to release 1,200 Turkish prisoners of war at the very start of the Napoleonic Era (1799-1815). France had just lost control of Egypt to the British and they were attempting to regroup to hold off the advancing British Navy. That's when Napoleon is said to have uttered the words, "*Ma sacrée toux.*" ("My damned cough.")

In a catastrophic misinterpretation, one officer heard "*Massacrez tous,*" ("Massacre them all,"). This supposedly resulted in every last prisoner being executed.

DEADLY LEAD SALTS USED AS WINE SWEETENERS

■ These days, artificial sweeteners have become part of our daily diets, but back in the age of the Ancient Romans, such a thing was new, exciting and deliciously fashionable. Lead acetate, sometimes known as 'sugar of lead', was a salt commonly used to sweeten the natural bitterness of wine. It's doubtful the use of lead in winemaking caused the fall of the empire, but considering how much grape flowed in Roman cups it wouldn't be a surprise if lead poisoning had been common among the thirstier members of society.

Sugar of lead continued to be used in winemaking for centuries, and it went on to claim the life of Pope Clement II, a papal head who enjoyed more than a sackful of wine. Some historians even believe sugar of lead caused the death of composer Beethoven.

SPORTS, ART & ENTERTAINMENT

121

114

127

CIRCUS STALLIONS DIVE FOR AN AUDIENCE

■ **Diving horse exhibitions were all the rage in late-19th and early-20th century USA and Canada.** Crowds would gather to see a mare and its rider plunge into water from an 18-metre-high ramp. The shows' popularity declined sharply due to animal welfare concerns after rumours surfaced over the use of electrical jolts to convince the horses to jump.

© Corbis

BARBIE'S 2,000-YEAR-OLD PREDECESSOR

■ **The rag doll is among the oldest toys discovered, with a few surviving Roman examples dating from the early centuries CE.** These dolls were made from coarse linen stuffed with rags and papyrus, with coloured wool used to create hair, as well as wood and clay to create any accompanying shoes and accessories. Historians believe these dolls would have been widespread in Ancient Egypt, Greece and Rome, but due to the perishable nature of their construction materials, not many have survived for excavation today.

A linen rag doll dating from Roman times

ROMANS KILLED TIME WITH BRUTAL AMUSEMENTS

Purging at feasts
Wealthy Romans loved their food so much that when they were full, they would induce vomiting so they could continue eating. This was considered a part of fine dining, and slaves were present to clear up sick that surfaced during the feast.

Slave abuse
As slaves were regarded as property, Roman law didn't view slave sex as infidelity. Seen as having 'no persona', Roman slaves would be sold at auctions or in shops. The buyer could even return a slave within six months for a refund.

Lewd graffiti
Experts were surprised by the amount of graffiti scrawled on the walls of Pompeii. The messages include boasting, insults and profanities, such as "Phileros is a eunuch", "Celadus makes the girls moan" and "The boss isn't worth a rat's ass!"

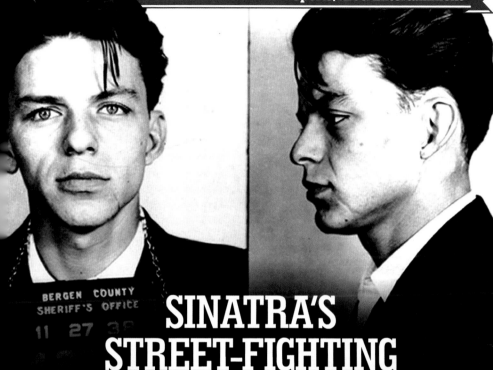

BERGEN COUNTY
SHERIFF'S OFFICE
11 27 38

SINATRA'S STREET-FIGHTING STREAK

Assault
In 1947, while having dinner at Ciro's in Los Angeles, Sinatra allegedly punched newspaper columnist Lee Mortimer, who had made a reference to his Italian ancestry and links with the Mafia. It was reported that Sinatra paid $9,000 to settle the case.

Dodging the draft
A persistent rumour suggested that Sinatra had paid a $40,000 bribe to doctors in New Jersey to be declared unfit for service during World War II. While his peers went and fought for the Allies in Europe and Asia, he lived the high life of a superstar. FBI files released in 1998 revealed that Sinatra had been legitimately rejected due to a perforated eardrum and 'mental instability', but the myth still prevails.

Adultery
In 1938, before Sinatra became famous, he was caught in a compromising position with a married woman in north New Jersey. At the time adultery was illegal, but he escaped a $500 fine when the charges were dropped.

Street fights
Sinatra admitted in later life that he had seen plenty of delinquent juvenile action. His teeth, he said, were straightened not by a dentist but in a punch-up, and the scar above his nose was from a Coke bottle being smashed in his face

Getty Images

SPORTS THAT SPILLED BLOOD FOR FUN

■ **It's not uncommon to see a bloody nose or two when watching contact sports like rugby.** But these sports are a whole different story, where spilling blood was often the aim of the game.

Cock-fighting
1646 - present day

Still legal in some countries, cockfighting is an enduringly popular blood sport. Before stepping into the fighting pit, the roosters have their beaks filed down and their wings clipped. To add to the bloodshed, spurs are attached to the cocks' claws, enabling them to mortally wound their opponent. Up to 32 chickens can do battle at one time and the sport has a huge gambling industry.

'Gamecocks' are specially bred for cockfighting

Octopus wrestling
20th century

In the 1960s, Americans watched in their thousands as divers wrestled molluscs to the ground. The sport was particularly popular on the west coast and involved divers searching for octopuses more than 15 metres below the surface. The fierce battle would usually culminate with the victorious diver bringing the exhausted octopus to the surface, but only after an almighty tussle.

Bare-knuckle boxing
17th century - present day

Bare-knuckle boxing took off in England in the 17th century. Wrestling holds were limited and hitting a downed opponent was forbidden. After a period of decline, new rules were introduced, and by the latter part of the 19th century, matches had become more organised occasions rather than unplanned scraps. Breaks between rounds were only 30 seconds long and the fights were tough endurance tasks. With no gloves, hands were often broken after landing a blow, so knockout punches were much less common than in modern boxing. Famous champs include John Gully, Tom Cribb, Jem Belcher and John L Sullivan.

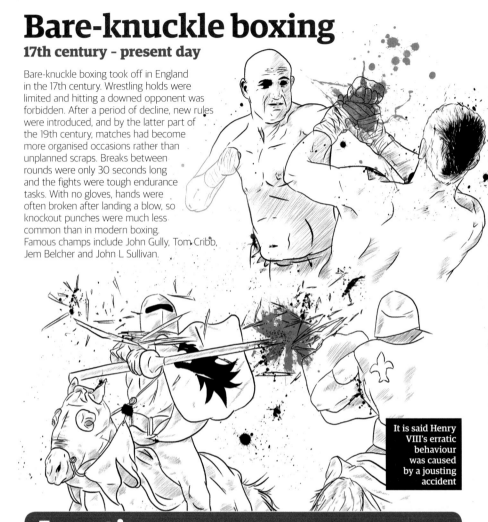

It is said Henry VIII's erratic behaviour was caused by a jousting accident

Jousting 11th-17th century

Initially a military exercise, jousting soon became a form of entertainment in the Middle Ages. Tournaments, or tourneys, were meticulously planned to best show off the talents of the knights. On horseback, two men would charge at each other at high speed with blunt, four-metre-long lances. If the first clash didn't end in a broken lance or one of the knights being unseated, they would race again until three lances had been broken or a knights hit the ground. Expert horsemanship and lance control were integral to victory.

The victor would claim prize money as well as his defeated foe's armour and horse. Veteran jousters would even travel to other parts of the country to face off against new opponents and enhance their reputation. Spectators would watch from a raised grandstand or from the castle itself. After the bloodshed had ended, it was off to feast and dance the night away.

FIRST PARACHUTER DIES IN EIFFEL TOWER JUMP

◼ **The unfortunate case of Franz Reichelt has gone down in history as a lesson in how not to test an invention.** Reichelt's idea of constructing a suit that would allow the wearer to glide through the air led him to experiment with various forms of cloth to create a parachute. He decided to test his invention by leaping off the Eiffel Tower to prove to the world that his device would deliver him to earth safely. It was an ambitious bid for immortality.

He had invited the press to attend, including one of the world's first film crews, who managed to capture what happened next. As he jumped off the tower the cloth folded around him, bundling him up, and he plummeted head first to the ground.

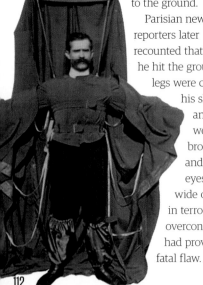

Parisian news reporters later recounted that after he hit the ground his legs were crushed, his skull and spine were broken and his eyes were wide open in terror. His overconfidence had proved his fatal flaw.

MAGICIAN'S BULLET TRICK GOES AWRY

◼ **The most dangerous trick in the history of magic is the bullet catch, having caused more casualties and deaths than any other.** A bullet is loaded into a gun and fired at the magician, who catches it in their hand or teeth. Numerous performers have been killed during this trick, but one in particular has become infamous.

Chung Ling Soo was an American man who adopted the persona of a Chinese magician. He never broke character or spoke English on stage, even going as far as using as interpreter when being interviewed. While performing the bullet catch in London in 1918, the gun had not been cleaned out properly and the bullet was launched into his chest.

For the first time ever, Ling Soo broke character, saying: "Oh my god, bring down the curtain. Something has happened." He died the next day.

ROALD DAHL SEDUCED WOMEN FOR THE CIA

■ The children's author who wrote *The BFG* and *Matilda* had a much more X-rated job during World War II. Before the United States joined the war, Dahl was recruited to sleep with high-society women.

After being shot down as a Royal Air Force fighter pilot over Libya in 1940, sustaining a fractured skull and temporary blindness, Dahl was rendered unable to fly. In 1942, he was transferred to a desk job at the British Embassy in Washington DC. However, he proved so popular with high-society ladies there that British Intelligence quickly found another role for him: seducing women and using them to promote Britain's interests in the United States.

This chiefly meant combating the America First movement, which was reluctant to join the war in Europe. He is known to have had an affair with Millicent Rogers, the heiress to a Standard Oil fortune, and formed friendships with many other prominent public figures, including vice president Henry Wallace and Charles Marsh, a self-made Texan newspaper magnate.

However, Dahl didn't always enjoy his unique mission. Clare Booth Luce, a prominent US Congresswoman and isolationist who was married to *Time* magazine founder Henry Luce, was reportedly so frisky in the bedroom that Dahl begged to be let off the assignment.

© Corbis

113

DR ZEUSS BOOKS BANNED UNDER MAO

■ **The founding father of the People's Republic of China was a tyrant ruler for over three decades.** In Mao's China, 'political correctness' was used by the state's legislature to control, repress and bully its population, with often absurdly counter-productive consequences. Besides the fear-inducing actions that were used, a number of bizarre measures were taken to control the people's behaviour...

New Year celebrations
The festivities were banned in 1967, during the darkest days of the revolution, on the grounds that the people needed to "change customs".

Dr Seuss
Or more specifically, Green Eggs And Ham for its "portrayal of early Marxism." However, how such connections could have been drawn is anyone's guess!

Cosmetics
Along with perfume, makeup was banned because it didn't conform to the "ideology of the collective proletariat" (in other words, encourage individual expression).

Golf
This pastime was banned almost as soon as Chairman Mao came to power. He officially outlawed it on the grounds that it was "a sport for millionaires."

Pets

A symbol of bourgeois decadence, owning a pet dog was against the law. Dogs were smuggled out of the country, or eaten by an undernourished populace. Dogs practically disappeared from China during this time.

The Sound Of Music

All Hollywood films were banned under Mao, including the famous 1965 musical starring Julie Andrews. Not that the ban stopped Madame Mao from singing along. A huge fan of the film, she would watch it in her private screening room.

Gambling

Betting was considered a hugely destructive vice and was banned in 1949. In 1957, his government created the re-education through labour programme that was, in part, used to punish gamblers.

The Beatles

While the rest of the world was enjoying it, the works of Lennon and McCartney – like all Western rock music – were banned from the airwaves for being symbolic of "bourgeois western decadence."

Mozart

Along with Bach, Beethoven and all the great classical composers, Mozart's music was outlawed in Mao's China. The crime? Being written in a pre-revolutionary time and society.

Sparrows

Huge numbers were culled in 1958 due to concerns that they ate too much of the rice harvest. Without sparrows, however, China's locust population boomed, harvests were wiped out and millions starved.

TRAPPED CLIMBER ESCAPES VIA SELF-AMPUTATION

An experienced climber, Aron Ralston believed he could conquer anything Utah's Blue John Canyon could throw at him. On 26 April 2003, that belief was tested to the extreme. During a descent of a narrow chasm, a 360-kilogram boulder came loose and landed on his arm, pinning him to a wall. The stricken adventurer spent five days trying to hack at the boulder before deciding desperate measures were required to stay alive. Finishing off his last gulp of water, he brandished his now blunt penknife and embarked on his last resort: cutting his arm off.

Ralston began the excruciating procedure by making a tourniquet from a pair of biking shorts to help stem the inevitable blood loss. The first step was to break the bones in his forearm; he had to snap his radius and then his ulna by contorting himself around the boulder. In agonising pain, he continued to amputate his arm, hacking away at what was left with his dull blade. After an hour, he was finally free.

He made it to the bottom of the canyon, collected some water and began hiking back to civilisation. He was later found by two Dutch tourists who helped him reach a helicopter that whisked him away to hospital. Aron Ralston was finally safe after what must have been one of the most painful ordeals imaginable.

© Alamy

WOMEN'S FOOTBALL BANNED FOR 50 YEARS

■ As women rallied together during the First World War, working together in large numbers, social and sporting events began to spring up. Of all the social gatherings, football became really popular. Factory bosses actively encouraged sport, as it improved the workers' health and wellbeing.

What was a friendly pastime soon became competitive, and several teams were formed. One of the most famous was Dick, Kerr's Ladies FC, who played in Preston. Formed in 1917, the club drew a crowd of 10,000 people for their first match. Later that year, the Munitionettes cup was won by Blyth Spartans, with striker Bella Reay scoring a hat-trick. The women's game reached a peak when 54,000 spectators crammed into Goodison Park on Boxing Day 1920.

Sadly, women's football was banned in 1921, when women were expected to return to the household. Despite its wartime popularity, women's football would not officially return until the ban was lifted 50 years later, in 1971.

© Thinkstock

GREEK METHOD MAN STEALS THE SHOW

■ While the Greeks famously invented theatre, most actors did not win any celebrity status until the fourth century BCE. One of the most popular was Polus.

Little is known about any of these actors today, but enough has been written about Polus to make him seem like an intriguing character. Some 2,300 years before 'the Method' was invented, he was perhaps the first method actor, using techniques that would put Brando or Newman to shame.

In the title role of Sophocles' *Elektra*, he wanted to faithfully portray emotion when Elektra received the urn with her brother's ashes. Even in Greek theatre, male actors would play female roles - a tradition that would continue until after Shakespeare's time. In an act of true dedication, Polus is said to have borrowed the ashes of his own recently deceased son from the tomb. With these ashes, tears must have flowed freely.

It is a legendary tale, and - if indeed it is true - one of the few anecdotes known about any actor of the Ancient Greek stage.

HARRY HOUDINI BRAINSTORMS HIS CV

Film star

Houdini's film career began as a way to show his outdoor escapes as part of his stage show, but grew quickly. His first starring role was in a serial called *The Master Mystery* and from there followed films such as *The Grim Game*, *Terror Island*, *The Man From Beyond* and *Haldane Of The Secret Service*. Houdini's film success could never match up with his affection for magic, and in 1923, he bowed out of the movie business altogether.

Aviator

Just after 1900, Houdini was gripped by a fascination with flight, and purchased a French biplane in 1909. He became a competent pilot and flew around Australia, intending to be the first person in the country to do so. Then it came to light that a Mr Defries from London had already pipped him to the post three months before. Never one to do things by halves, Houdini didn't fly his plane again.

Spy

In 2006, the book *The Secret Life Of Houdini* claimed Houdini was a spy for Britain and the US in WWI. Houdini could speak German, which would have been essential, and authors William Kalush and Harry Sloman argued Houdini spied on political leaders and royalty, using his career as a cover. The link was made when they found a diary written by William Melville, a British spymaster, which mentioned Houdini.

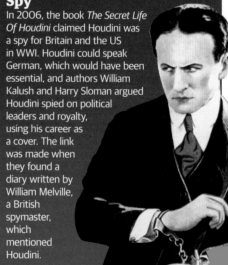

© Alamy

KIM JONG-IL WAS A HOLLYWOOD FANATIC

■ **Kim Jong-il was a huge film fan, and while he despised America, he had a penchant for Hollywood movies.** He loved James Bond and had a fondness for Elizabeth Taylor. He wrote a book about cinema and he amassed a collection of 20,000 films. More than that, he became involved in film-making too.

Sea Of Blood was his triumph, a war epic set during the Japanese occupation of Korea in the 1930s. Official accounts describe how Jong-il trusted writers to come up with a screenplay but would, using his 'genius' and clarity of thought, perfect the script. He oversaw its production as co-director.

Such was his love of cinema that he went as far as kidnapping two of South Korean cinema's most famous names - directors Shin Sang-ok and Choi Eun-hee - in 1978. They were treated well, in separate houses, but they were taught the ideology of the Great Leader. Shin tried to escape twice and was tortured, required to sit up straight, cross-legged for hours at a time, fed little and forced to write a letter of apology to Kim Jong-il. Five years later, the pair were reunited and they went on to make seven films for Kim Jong-il who spent millions, sparing no expense in the pursuit of his film-making dreams.

© Thinkstock

119

LAST SUPPER SURVIVES AGAINST THE ODDS

■ **Unusually for a piece of art, Leonardo da Vinci's *Last Supper* was thought of as a masterpiece in the artist's own lifetime.** But within a few years of completion it was already flaking away, thanks to the way da Vinci had created it. To form a traditional fresca he would have had to paint quickly on damp plaster, but he didn't like to rush, so he used a slower oil and tempura over dry plaster method. This meant the painting was never properly fixed to the surface.

In 1652, it suffered a different sort of calamity when a group of friars decided to have a door put through the middle of the wall supporting the painting, obliterating Christ's legs for good.

Early attempts to save the picture were horribly botched, involving everything from alcohol to caustic soda. In 1821, an artist called Stefano Barezzi decided to take all the paint off and mount it on canvas instead. When he realised that he was destroying the *Last Supper*, Barezzi gave up and haplessly tried to glue the pieces back on.

In 1796, when Napoleon marched triumphantly into Milan, French troops were billeted at the convent. The room housing the *Last Supper* became a stable and soldiers used the painting for target practice. But the *Last Supper*'s biggest threat occurred when Mussolini's Italy entered WWII and Milan was targeted by Allied bombers on around 50 occasions. On the night of 16 August 1943, a ten-ton bomb landed on the convent. Remarkably, the painting remained intact, sandbags having protected it from shrapnel.

CHARLIE CHAPLIN'S THREE TEEN WIVES

■ **It may come as a surprise, but there was a darker side to Chaplin's unparalleled fame.** He gained notoriety for his string of short-lived marriages - and for the average age of his wives. His first, actress Mildred Harris, was only 17 years old (Chaplin was 29) when they were hastily hitched in 1918, prompted by a pregnancy scare. They divorced in 1920.

Four years later Chaplin quietly married another teen actress, the 16-year-old Lita Grey. This time the pregnancy was genuine. Their son, Charles Jr, was born six months later, but Grey's 1926 application for divorce cited Chaplin's infidelity, abuse and "perverted sexual desires."

His third wife, Paulette Goddard (yet another actress), was 21 when they began their relationship in 1932. They were married in 1937 but separated a year later. After that, in 1943, he married the 18-year old Oona O'Neill. Chaplin himself was 54 by this point, and embroiled in a paternity suit with the 23-year-old actress Joan Barry.

His relationship with Barry had seen him fall foul of the Mann Act, and old law that prohibiting "the transportation of women across state boundaries for sexual purposes." He was acquitted but admonished by the judge for "moral turpitude".

MAYAN LOSERS FACED DECAPITATION

■ **A common feature of many Mayan towns, great masonry structures hosted grand feasts, rituals and wrestling matches.** However, their primary purpose and most popular attraction was the deadly Mayan ball game of pok-ta-pok.

When the ancient game was played, the stone slabs transformed into a battleground, a sacred place, a portal between this world and the one beyond. Two opposing teams would face each other with the aim of keeping the ball in play and, for an instant win, directing the ball through a high mounted vertical hoop. The players could only use their hips, shoulders, head and knees as the use of feet or hands was forbidden.

Players would dash around the court with lighting-quick speed in an attempt to lead their team to victory, as a single wrong move could mean the difference between life and death.

01

1. The ball court
Ball courts were built in an 'I' shape with a long narrow alley flanked by sloping walls with enclosed end-zones. The Chichen Itza ball court was a massive 96.5 x 30m (316.6 x 98.4ft).

03

2. Uniform
Players would traditionally wear loincloths with leather hip guards. A thick wood or wicker girdle that would also help to propel the ball with more force. Elaborate ceremonial headdresses were also worn, though likely only for special, ritual occasions.

3. Steep steps
Steps were a backdrop in many murals. They could have played a part in a separate game, or used in the human sacrifice ceremonies following some games.

6. Stone rings

If the ball passed through one of the vertical stone rings, a decisive victory was awarded to the scoring team. However, the rings were barely bigger than the ball and were set high above the playing field – for example 6m (19.6ft) at Chichen Itza.

4. Artwork

The walls of the court were plastered and brightly painted, featuring many stone reliefs. They told tales of games played in the arena, as well as scenes of captives and sacrifice.

06

04

05

02

5. Rubber ball

Solid rubber balls were used in the game, usually made from latex of the rubber tree. They were so heavy that the players risked serious injury or even death if struck by them. Evidence shows skulls were also used as balls.

ASHES CRICKET SERIES NAMED IN JEST

■ **England's cricketing past is a long and glorious one.** The first documented game took place in Guildford in the 16th century, and, thanks to the British Empire, its popularity spread across the globe.

Before long, international teams began to rival the home one, and England lost their first home series in 1882 during the ninth Test match against Australia.

A mock obituary appeared in *The Sporting Times*, which read: "In Affectionate Remembrance of ENGLISH CRICKET, which died at the Oval on 29th AUGUST, 1882, Deeply lamented by a large circle of sorrowing friends and acquaintances R.I.P. N.B. - The body will be cremated and the ashes taken to Australia."

As a result, the English captain Ivo Bligh dubbed the 1882-83 tour, "The quest to regain the ashes." His mission was successful, and during a private match that was played over Christmas 1882, the Australian team were defeated.

The wife of Sir William Clark, who had hosted the game, found a small wooden urn, burned a cricket pail, and placed the ashes inside before presenting it to Bligh.

In Affectionate Remembrance
OF
ENGLISH CRICKET,
WHICH DIED AT THE OVAL
ON
29th AUGUST, 1882,
Deeply lamented by a large circle of sorrowing friends and acquaintances.

R. I. P.

N.B.—The body will be cremated and the ashes taken to Australia.

The prize in 1883 was an urn holding the 'ashes' of English cricket

WARTIME TRUCE TO BOOST OLYMPICS ATTENDANCE

■ **Dating back millennia, the Olympic Truce was started in the 9th century BCE by Olympians in a bid to ensure peace during the games.** It's a tradition that was revived in the 1990s that sees warfare halted for the duration of the games to enable spectators to attend the event. Most remarkably, in the 2000 Sydney summer games, both South and North Korea united under one banner in the opening ceremony - the first time in the Olympics the two halves stood as one country.

VAN GOGH ONLY SOLD ONE PAINTING

■ **You might consider Van Gogh to be one of the most famous artists to date, but in his time he was one of many relatively unknown artists in France.** In fact, he only ever sold one painting during his lifetime: *The Red Vineyard*, created in 1888. In 1890 Russian art collector Sergei Shchukin bought the work for approximately 400 francs. Van Gogh killed himself just a few months later. These days audiences can view the masterpiece at the Pushkin Museum of Fine Arts in Moscow.

POE'S CANNIBAL PROPHECY COMES TRUE

▣ **In 1838, Edgar Allan Poe published his only complete novel, *The Narrative Of Arthur Gordon Pym Of Nantucket.* In it, the** young Pym stows away in a whaling ship called Grampus. At sea, a storm breaks the mast, leaving the crew shipwrecked and facing starvation. With no land in sight, crew member Richard Parker suggests one of them be sacrificed to feed the others. They draw straws and Parker is killed and eaten. An eerie tale - even for a fiction. Then, around 50 years later, the events of the novel came true.

In 1884, the Mignonette set sail from England to Australia carrying a crew of four: Tom Dudley, Edwin Stephens, Edmund Brooks and 17-year-old Richard Parker. Just off the Cape of Good Hope, the ship was caught in a storm and sank, leaving them stranded in a lifeboat. The crew decided one of them should be sacrificed, and Parker was selected as he was unwell.

After their rescue, the criminal case became one of history's most infamous; it helped outlaw survival cannibalism and also granted Poe's story a prophetic quality.

TRADE UNIONS PROTECT GLADIATORS' RIGHTS

■ **Think of a Roman gladiator and you'll imagine a man fighting for his life every night, battling fellow warriors and wild animals for the entertainment of the paying public.** Much of that was true; the enslaved fighters were more than bloodthirsty playthings, they were almost a class of their own. It was a class that knew its worth in the fighting pit. As such, gladiators were known to form unions or 'collegia' to create a greater sense of unity among their number. For instance, gladiators would elect their own leaders, worship their own deities (Rome was polytheistic prior to the rise of Christianity) and perform their own funeral rites in the event of a gladiator's death.

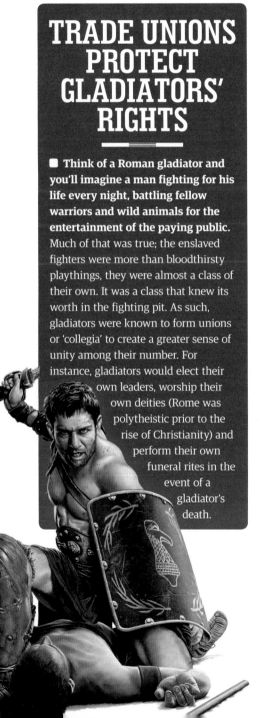

MARK TWAIN'S HALLEY'S COMET COINCIDENCE

■ **On 30 November 1835, celebrated American author Samuel Langhorne Clemens (known professionally as Mark Twain) was born on the same day that Halley's comet crossed paths with the world.** The cosmological phenomenon only occurs every 17 years, making it a very rare event indeed.

By 1909 – a good 74 years later – Twain would offer a hauntingly accurate prediction: he'd die on the day Halley's Comet returned, just as he entered the world alongside it. He was even quoted as saying, "It will be the greatest disappointment of my life if I don't go out with Halley's Comet. The Almighty has said, no doubt: 'Now here are these two unaccountable freaks; they came in together, they must go out together'."

He was right. Twain died of a heart attack on 21 April 1910, a day after the reappearance of Halley's Comet.

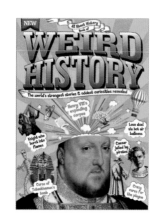

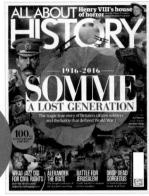